CHILDISH THINGS

LOUISE BOURGEOIS
HELEN CHADWICK
ROBERT GOBER
SUSAN HILLER
MIKE KELLEY
JEFF KOONS
PAUL McCARTHY

CHILDISH THINGS

DAVID HOPKINS

PUBLISHED BY
THE FRUITMARKET GALLERY
45 Market Street
Edinburgh, EH1 1DF

Telephone +44 (0)131 225 2383
Facsimile: +44 (0)131 220 3130
www.fruitmarket.co.uk

ON THE OCCASION OF THE EXHIBITION
CHILDISH THINGS
19 November 2010 - 23 January 2011

Curated by David Hopkins

ISBN 978-0-947912-94-9

Publishing is an intrinsic part of The Fruitmarket Gallery's creative programme, with books published to accompany each exhibition. Books are conceived as part of the exhibition-making process, with the book extending the reach and life of each exhibition and offering artists and curators a second space in which to present their work.

The Fruitmarket Gallery is a not-for-profit organisation and a Scottish charity presenting world-class, challenging art made by Scottish and international artists in an environment that is welcoming, engaging, informative and always free.

The Gallery is Foundation Funded by Creative Scotland for up to 58% of its running costs and must raise additional funds to support its exhibitions, education and publishing programmes.

The Fruitmarket Gallery is a company limited by guarantee, registered in Scotland No. 87888 and registered as a Scottish Charity No. SC 005576 Registered Office: 45 Market St., Edinburgh, EH1 1DF VAT No. 398 2504 21

CONTENTS

FOREWORD

FIONA BRADLEY

This publication marks The Fruitmarket Gallery's second collaboration with David Hopkins, Professor of Art History at the University of Glasgow; acknowledged authority on Marcel Duchamp, dada and surrealism; increasingly renowned writer on contemporary art; and curator of the thought-provoking and popular 2006 exhibition 'Dada's Boys: Identity and Play in Contemporary Art' for The Fruitmarket Gallery.

We are proud to welcome David back to the Gallery in the context of this new exhibition and publication, 'Childish Things'. Like 'Dada's Boys' before it, 'Childish Things' has its origins in dada and surrealism, but this new exhibition includes no dada or surrealist art. Rather, it looks at a post-dada/surrealist interest in toys as signifiers of what David terms a 'dark poetics' of childhood, bringing together the work of seven senior and historically significant artists from Britain and the United States. As always in David's exhibitions, each work by each artist has been carefully chosen for its relevance to, and illumination of his initial line of enquiry – each work speaks volumes, of childhood and its related anxieties, and of the power of art to make a context in which to think ideas through. The works displayed in the exhibition and discussed in this publication are major works by artists at the top of their game: they react with each other and with the theme of the exhibition, but are in no way confined, brimming over with meanings too complex to sit easily in anyone's box. 'Childish Things' celebrates their independent force as much as the way in which they may be brought together.

We are grateful to David for his ideas, enthusiasm and interest in and commitment to The Fruitmarket Gallery. We thank the lenders to the exhibition, both public and private, and our partners in the artists' galleries and studios who have worked with us to bring these extraordinary works to Edinburgh. Unashamed champions of the impact of objects in space, we are delighted to offer our audience the chance to encounter sculptures and projections of this calibre at The Fruitmarket Gallery. As always, however, it is to the artists that we owe the greatest debt of gratitude – for making the work, and for entrusting it to us.

INTRODUCTION

TOYS FOR ADULTS

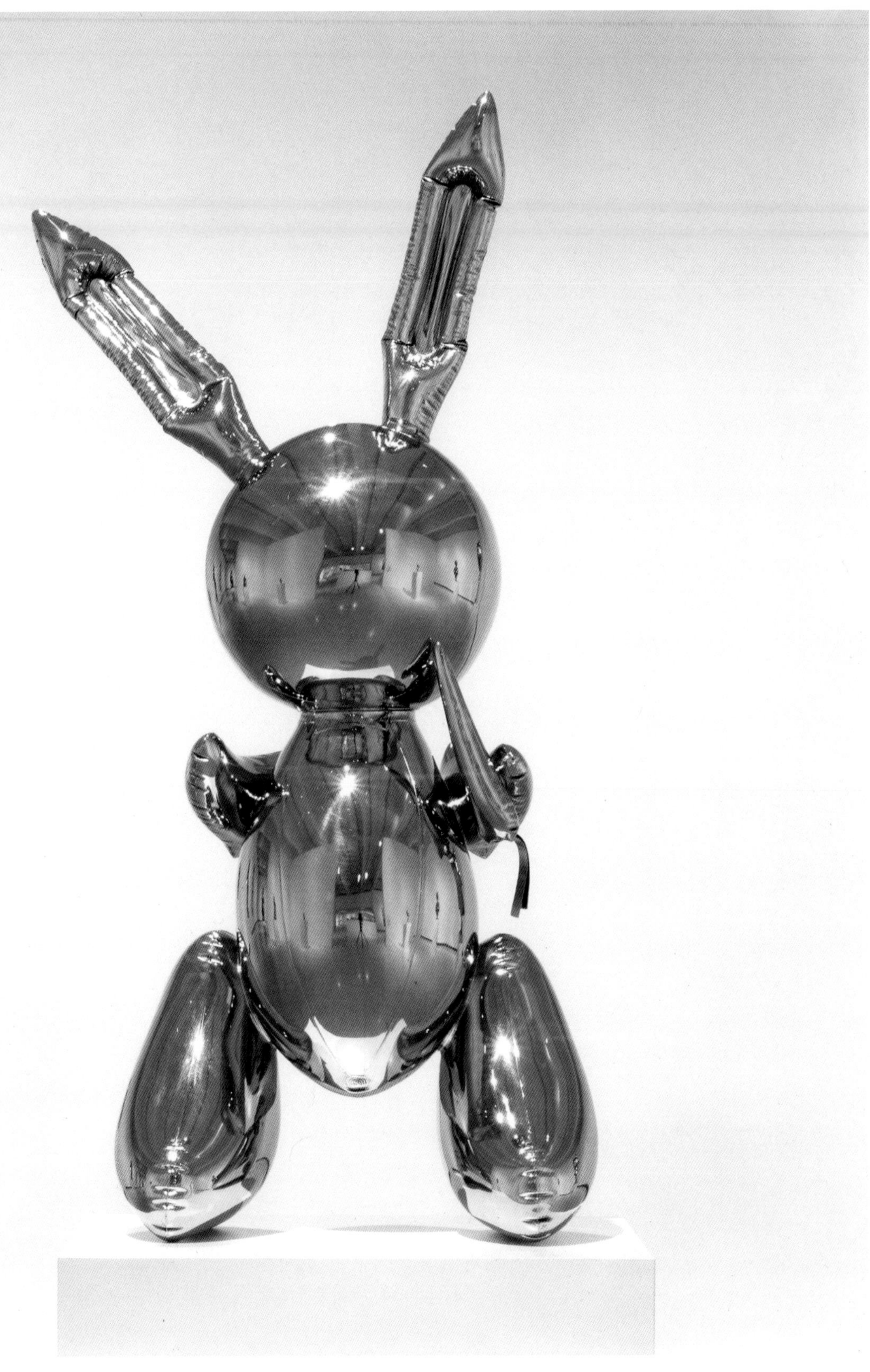

JEFF KOONS, *Rabbit*, 1986

'Childish Things' is an exhibition at The Fruitmarket Gallery in Edinburgh which seeks to explore the relationship between art, attitudes to childhood and the iconography of play in a new and metaphorically open-ended way. Its historical focus is highly specific. It examines art produced in a twenty-five-year period between 1983 and 2008 in Britain and the US, so that a set of themes can emerge from work which was produced in fairly homogeneous social and artistic conditions. The exhibition includes a major video installation and a film, which work in dialogue with one another and set the tone, but the emphasis is largely on sculpture/objects. These sit around the Gallery like over-sized playthings in a child's room.

Many of the iconic images in the art of the late-twentieth century were toys. Consider, for instance, Jeff Koons's *Rabbit* of 1986, a sculpture of an inflatable toy rabbit in stainless steel. But surprisingly few exhibitions so far seem to have looked at the idea of toys, toy-like objects or playthings as subjects in the art of the recent past. Possibly part of the reason is precisely the slippage from 'toys' to 'playthings' that occurred in the last sentence. The fact is that aesthetically-produced objects, which arise from processes that are frequently seen as analogous to play, often avoid referencing toys in an overly-direct manner.[1] There are obvious exceptions to this. One could think of many instances of Pop Art (particularly Peter Blake) or of the so-called Appropriation Art of the 1980s (especially Koons) where the toy is often adopted as a readymade or pre-given image. Often, however, the object that appears in art as a consequence of an encounter with toys is more enigmatic in its reference. It may have something broader to say about childhood, or about nostalgia, regression, or other such related ideas. It may look toy-like, but it is rarely a literal reference to a toy: a toy car, say, or a teddy bear.

So what is a toy? When we delve deeper into the idea of toys, it becomes clear that they are rather unstable entities, historically speaking. The historian of childhood Philippe Ariès, while accepting the possibility of a seemingly logical evolution from adult-usage to child-usage in those objects we call toys ('some toys originated in that spirit of emulation which induces children to imitate adult processes, while reducing them to their own scale'[2]), goes on to despair of the difficulty of distinguishing between adult uses of miniaturised objects and children's toys.

> Historians of the toy, and collectors of dolls and toy miniatures, have always had considerable difficulty in separating the doll, the child's toy, from all the other images and statuettes which the sites of excavations yield up … and which more often than not had a religious significance: objects of a household or funerary cult, relics from a pilgrimage etc … I am not suggesting that in the past children did not play with dolls or replicas of adult belongings. But they were not the only ones to use these replicas; what in modern times was to become their monopoly, they had to share in ancient times, at least with the dead.[3]

This rather dark apprehension of the origins of toys and of their fundamental ambiguity has provoked a fascinating discussion by the Italian philosopher Giorgio Agamben, who enlists several other theorists to develop his ideas. One of these is the poet Rainer Maria Rilke who explores the essentially fetishistic logic of children's relations with toys. Rilke describes the terrible unresponsiveness of the child's doll to the efforts its owner makes to feed and water it (it is 'incapable of absorbing at any point even a single drop of water.') As a result, he argues 'that hatred that, unconscious, has always constituted a part of our relation to it, breaks forth: the doll lies before us unmasked like the horrible strange body on which we have dissipated our purest warmth.'[4]
The uncanny life of toys alluded to here, which crops up as a theme repeatedly in children's fiction – Pinocchio is just one example – is extended by Agamben into a discussion of the way in which toys elude any precise positioning in terms of our inner and outer worlds. Here Agamben references the work of the British psychologist Donald Woods Winnicott and his notion of the transitional object. Such an object, which exists as Winnicott suggestively remarks 'between the thumb and the teddy bear' and is likely to be a scrap of blanket or an early comforter, represents the child's first 'not me' object: the means by which an intermediate zone is initially established between the subjective and the objectively-perceived world.[5] Extrapolating from these ideas, Agamben concludes:

> Things are not outside of us, in measurable external space, like the neutral objects (*ob-jecta*) of use and exchange ... Like the fetish, like the toy, things are not properly anywhere, because their place is found on this side of objects and beyond the human in a zone that is no longer objective or subjective, neither personal nor impersonal, neither material nor immaterial, but where we find ourselves suddenly facing these apparently so simple unknowns: the human, the thing.[6]

It becomes evident, then, that toys, as objects which have always inhabited an ambiguous zone vis-à-vis the reality principle, serve adults, as much as children, as means of expressing anxieties, yearnings, fantasies and so forth, and have a direct relation to the artistic impulse. (The work of psychoanalysts such as Winnicott and Melanie Klein bears this out in abundance.[7]) If toys continue to serve adult needs (think of the miniature figurines or ornaments we place on our mantelpieces), adults nevertheless displace their own childishness onto their children, manufacturing toys as much to serve their own needs as those of their offspring – a good example is the commonplace of the father who plays with the toy aeroplane more than the son for whom it is bought. In a famous essay on toys, the critic Roland Barthes lamented the way in which adults devise ever more realistic toys with which to impose their own values onto their children:

> There exist, for instance, dolls which urinate; they have an oesophagus ... they wet their nappies ... This is meant to prepare the little girl for the causality of housekeeping, to 'condition' her ... However, faced with this world of faithful and complicated objects, the child can only identify himself as owner, as user, never as creator; he does not invent the world, he uses it.[8]

As is well known, children, left to their own devices, readily construct play-situations with the simplest objects (cardboard box and string) without any recourse to toys as such. The cultural historian of toys Brian Sutton-Smith makes the interesting point that the manufactured toy partly came into being to offset the solitariness of the modern child; to keep the child occupied in the absence of siblings or the social milieu of earlier times.[9] It seems, then, that it is adults, ironically, that toys are *for*. Despite St. Paul's famous designation of adulthood as the point at which 'childish things' are put away, the fact is that toys can never be relinquished. Once again, it is art itself which most obviously approaches the condition of the toy. For André Breton, the leader of the surrealist movement, Pablo Picasso was pre-eminently the creator of 'tragic toys for adults'. In a visionary statement on Picasso, Breton seems to ironically echo St. Paul: 'when we were children we had toys that would make us weep with pity and anger today. One day, perhaps, we shall see the toys of our whole life spread before us like those of our childhood.'[10]

'Childish Things' spreads out toy or play-related artworks of various kinds around The Fruitmarket Gallery. These objects and projected works can be seen either as metaphorically related to toys and childhood, or else as direct references to them. Scale is perhaps the unifying principle in this regard. All the works express something of importance with regard to this issue; they mostly play on an inversion of the scale we would expect from childish things (Helen Chadwick, Jeff Koons, Susan Hiller), but they also make use of miniaturisation (Louise Bourgeois) or else appropriate something of the child's own scale (Robert Gober, Mike Kelley). As in the perceptions of writers such as Rilke, Agamben or Winnicott, they are generally dark or perhaps skewed toys, speaking of the projection of adult needs onto the things of childhood. They speak of nostalgia, or self-discovery, or sometimes of a self-consciousness about the imposition of the adult onto the child's world via the commodity, or the need to protect or instruct. They are especially probing about the way we socialize children.

As for their actual relation to toys, each object speaks in a different register. Toys are actually absent – disturbingly so – from Robert Gober's playpen; they lie eviscerated on Mike Kelley's blanket. Helen Chadwick's toy-like objects suggest a giant's throw of the dice – human destiny laid out before us like the pieces of a game. Louise Bourgeois's Oedipus narrative suggests something similar, except the figures are shrunk to the size of a child's homemade figurines. Jeff Koons's massively enlarged knick-knacks suggest the adult commercialization of the child's viewpoint; Paul McCarthy's readymade anatomical aid comments wryly on toys as educational aids. Susan

Hiller's powerful video projection extends the idea of the toy to entertainment (commenting darkly on its adult implications). McCarthy's second readymade work in the exhibition, his re-playing of *The Sound of Music* backwards and upside-down, extends this idea but pointedly upends an adult conception of childhood and the saccharine 'Favourite Things' that are associated with it in mass culture. McCarthy's anarchic work also suggests a wilful regression to a destructive child-like state on the part of the artist, and several works in 'Childish Things' suggest a similar atavistic impulse; Kelley and McCarthy's pieces, for instance, powerfully revisit the urges of children to open up and investigate bodies.

The above ideas will be explored at length in the rest of this book, but it should further be noted that, in their plaything-like nature, the selected objects and projections circle around ideas of childhood in two interrelated ways. They tend either to recapitulate or work through episodes from the artists' own childhood (Bourgeois, Chadwick, Gober), in order to make broader points, or else they comment either obliquely or directly on the ways in which childhood and the child were understood, particularly in the world of the 1980s and 1990s (Hiller, Kelley, Koons, McCarthy).

The time frame of this exhibition leads me to make one final point about the curatorial rationale underpinning it. 'Childish Things' deals with the art of a quarter of a century, from Chadwick's *Ego Geometria Sum* (1983) to McCarthy's *cisuM fo dnuoS ehT / The Sound of Music* (2008), foregrounding, unapologetically, work by the leading figures of recent British and American art. This period, however, has not yet been understood in any conclusive way. 'Postmodernism' is now a term that has little critical currency, with many historians feeling happier to think of modernism as something that is far from over. The concept of 'globalization' describes a broad structural situation, but the attempt to identify a climate of feeling, or even a cultural dominant in the art of the last couple of decades – especially in the West – is hardly part of its remit. The concern of this exhibition is to examine how artworks of the period can be united, not by principles of style or theoretical allegiance, but by reflections, preoccupations and anxieties around the topos of childhood/toys; to draw out, in other words, why the nostalgic invocation of the child-self and its toys reveals some of the deeper-lying preoccupations of the age. Yet how do we account for this nostalgia, this return to the romantic signifier *par excellence*, the child? Should we understand this as a regressive indication, a turning backwards or inwards – a kind of *fin de siècle* phenomenon? Or is something more fundamental about our attitude to ourselves, our beliefs and our ethical responsibilities, being staked out on the terrain of childhood? This question lies behind the discussion that follows.

NOTES

1. The classic text on play and culture is Johan Huizinga, *Homo Ludens*, Roy Publishers, Boston, 1950.
2. Philippe Ariès, *Centuries of Childhood* (trans. Robert Baldrick), Paris, 1960, reprinted Peregrine Books, Harmondsworth, 1986, p. 65.
3. Ibid., pp. 66–7.
4. Rainer Maria Rilke as quoted by Giorgio Agamben, 'Mme Panckoucke; or, The Toy Fairy' in *Stanzas: Word and Phantasm in Western Culture* (trans. R. Martinez), University of Minnesota Press, Minneapolis, 1993, p. 57.
5. See D. W. Winnicott, *Playing and Reality*, London, 1971, reprinted Pelican, Harmondsworth, 1988, p. 2.
6. Agamben, op. cit., p. 59.
7. See, for instance, Melanie Klein, 'The Psychoanalytic Play Technique: Its History and Significance', 1955, in Juliet Mitchell (ed.), *The Selected Melanie Klein*, Peregrine Books, Harmondsworth, 1986, pp. 35–54.
8. Roland Barthes, 'Toys' in *Mythologies* (trans. A. Lavers), Paris, 1957, reprinted Granada, London, 1981, pp. 53–54.
9. Brian Sutton-Smith, *Toys as Culture*, Gardner Press, New York, 1986, see Chapter 3, pp. 23–41.
10. André Breton, 'Surrealism and Painting' Paris, 1928, reprinted in *Surrealism and Painting* (trans. Simon Watson Taylor), Icon Editions, New York, 1972, p. 6.

CHAPTER 1

ORIGINS

LOUISE BOURGEOIS AND HELEN CHADWICK

We were taught, in the mid-1980s, to distrust origins. In the brief heyday of postmodernism, the importation of post-structuralist theory from France made cultural commentators uneasy about 'essential' concepts – about origins, authenticity and so on. Outlining a philosophic rupture, Jacques Derrida wrote:

> This was a moment when ... in the absence of a centre or origin, everything became discourse ... that is to say, a system in which the central signified, the original or transcendental signified, is never absolutely present outside a system of differences.[11]

Looking at some of the most distinctive art of the 1980s now, it is noticeable that two of the main female practitioners of the period – Louise Bourgeois and the younger Helen Chadwick – do not fit easily under this kind of theoretical rubric. Their work is often explicitly concerned with the recovery of a 'centre or origin', or indeed with a *return to origins*. Rather than fitting neatly into a cultural category, they exemplify the psychological predisposition of art and the humanities in general in the 1980s and 1990s. This was a period when psychoanalysis, now fully professionalised, entered the broader academic sphere. In terms of art, it was a period that saw a work such as Mary Kelly's *Post Partum Document* (a complex investigation of the psychological relationship between the artist and her young son, which was published as a book in 1983) inspire numerous feminist art historians and critics to turn to Freud's post-structuralist exegete Jacques Lacan in order to explore concepts of gender formation. I will argue later that the psychologistic tenor of the advanced art of the times would engender a satirical reversal in the work of artists such as Mike Kelley and Paul McCarthy, who both confirm and react against psychoanalysis, specifically in its concern with childhood. It is within the climate of a widespread turn to the psychoanalytical, however, that the highly self-conscious attitudes to childhood and to origins were fostered in the late work of Bourgeois and the early work of Chadwick.

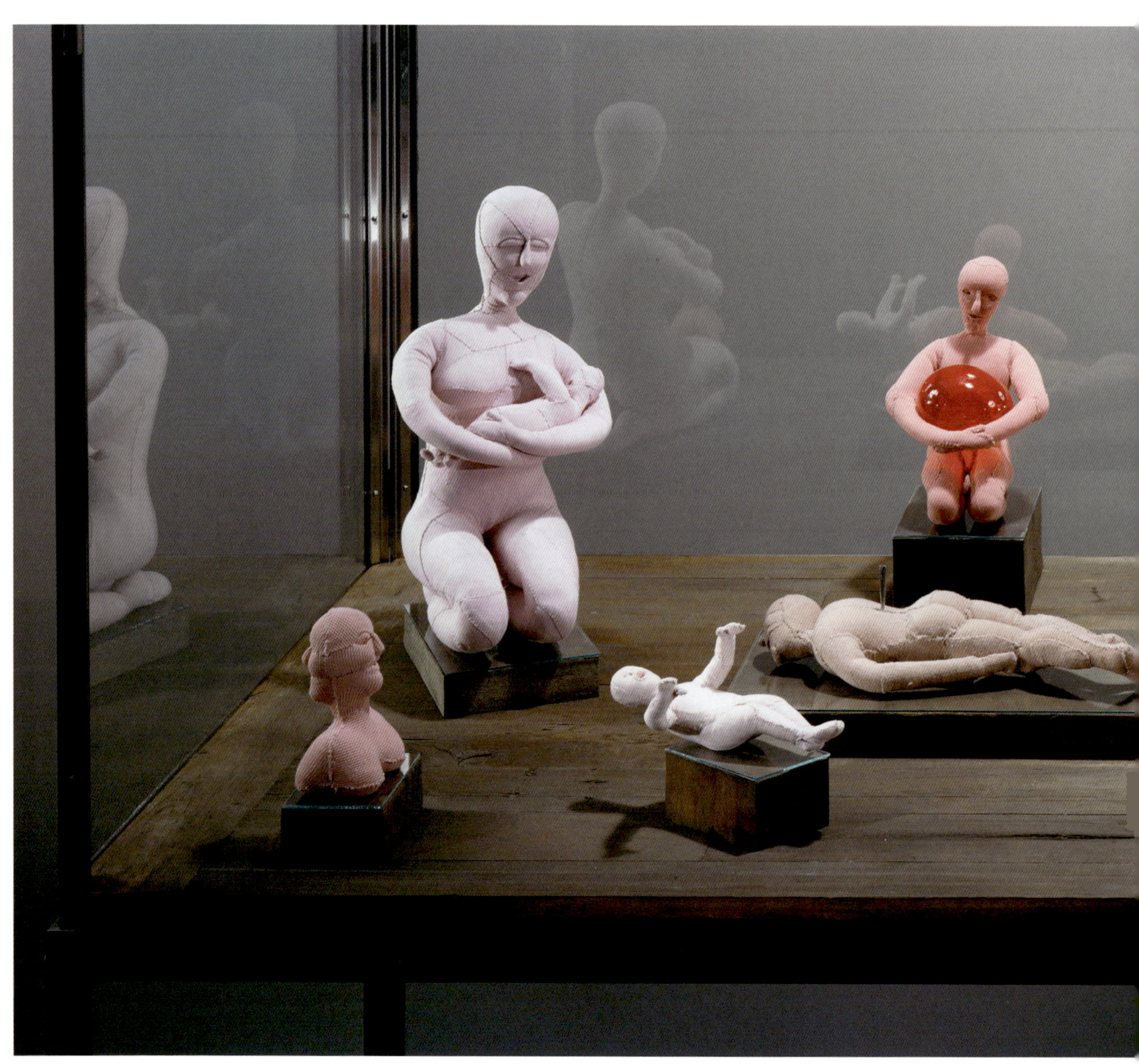

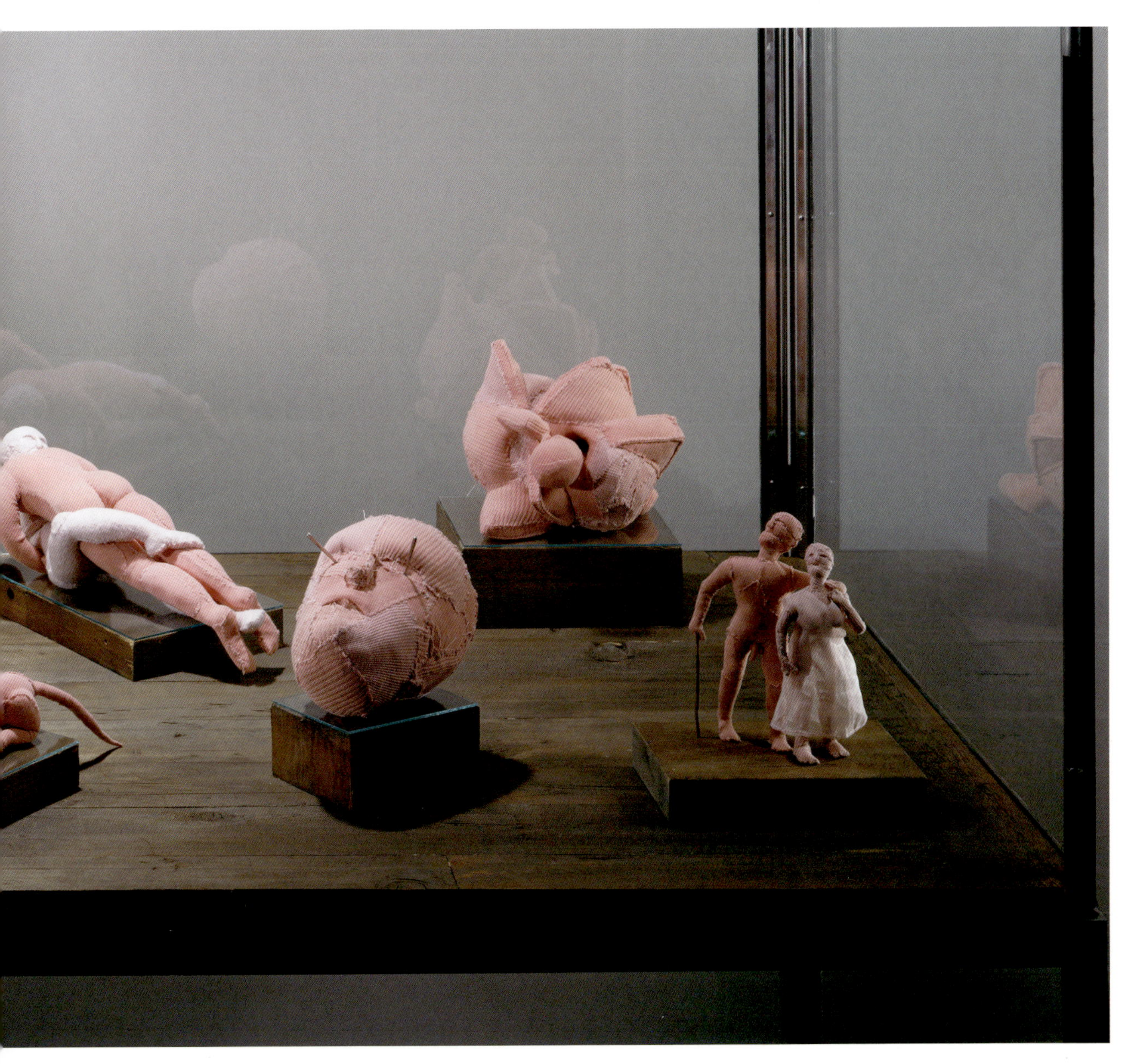

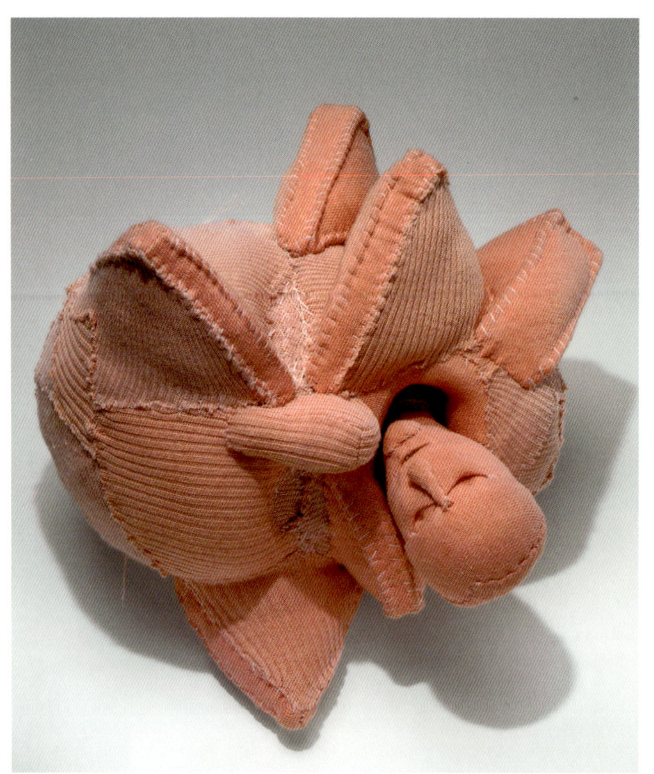
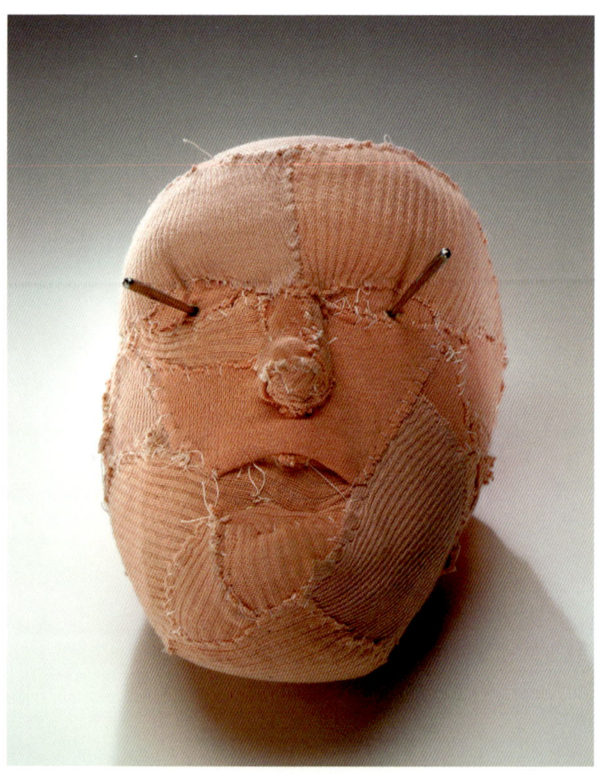
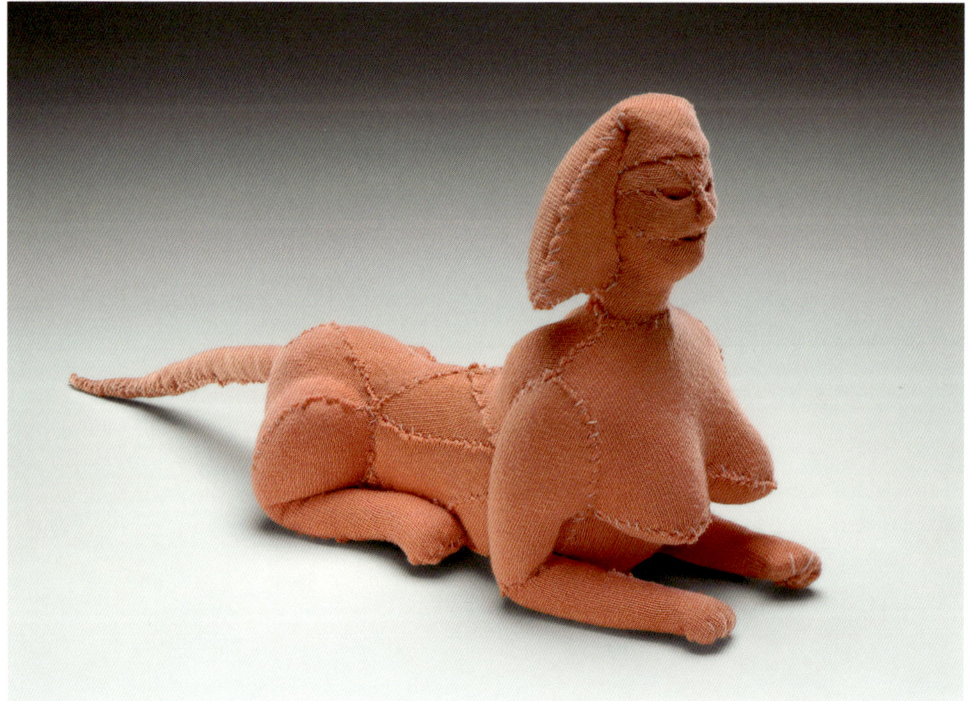

previous pages and opposite: LOUISE BOURGEOIS, *Oedipus*, 2003

FREUD'S TOYS

Louise Bourgeois's 2003 vitrine assemblage *Oedipus* thematises the concept of origins in exemplary fashion. Its subject, the story of Oedipus, which has been pieced together over time from various sources in Greek mythology, in itself represents an originary account of human development and destiny. To recount it briefly: Laius, King of Thebes, receives a prophecy that if a son should be born to himself and his wife, Jocasta, then he will be murdered by him. When Jocasta does indeed give birth to a son, who is named Oedipus, Laius has the baby's ankles pinned together so that he cannot crawl and abandons him on a mountain. His son, however, is rescued by a shepherd who gives the child to the King and Queen of Corinth to raise as their own. As a young man, Oedipus hears a rumour that he is not the biological son of the King and Queen, but when he asks them they deny the truth. Suspicious of their answer, Oedipus travels to the Oracle at Delphi, but the Oracle does not answer his question, instead telling him that he is destined to marry his mother and kill his father. Hearing this Oedipus leaves Corinth thinking he is avoiding his fate. Travelling towards Thebes he kills a man in a skirmish at a crossroad near the city, unaware that the man is his father, Laius. Arriving at the outskirts of Thebes Oedipus defeats the Sphinx by answering its riddle correctly, freeing the city from the monster. As a reward, he is offered the city's widowed Queen, Jocasta's, hand in marriage. Unwittingly, therefore, he fulfils the Oracle's prophecy by marrying his mother. Eventually the truth of what has happened emerges. Jocasta commits suicide, and Oedipus, in a fit of remorse, blinds himself. He leaves Thebes in exile, with his daughter Antigone acting as his guide as he blindly wanders the countryside.

It was this narrative, of course, or rather Sophocles' version of it in *Oedipus Rex*, that Freud drew on to develop his psychoanalytic notion of the Oedipus complex in the early-twentieth century. The prohibition against incest that underpins the Oedipus story, which was understood by Freud to exist universally, became for him one of the determining factors in the structure of the unconscious. All children, Freud's thesis went, unconsciously fantasise about the parent of the opposite sex as love objects and have to deal psychically with the terrible consequences of infringing the taboo. The successful surrender of the initial fantasy and the replacement of the fantasised parental object with a more socially acceptable love object is seen as necessary for normal development (although Freud's ideas of normalcy, to say nothing of the way his ideas were largely predicated on male psychic development, have been radically contested).

Turning now to Bourgeois, widely regarded as one of the foremost artists of the twentieth century (who died in May 2010 as this exhibition was being planned), it is significant that her work paradigmatically thematises the Freudian excavation of the unconscious, constantly reverting back to her own origins. Bourgeois, born in 1911, developed her artistic path in the context of surrealism; her sculptural work of the 1940s and 1950s can be indexed directly to surrealist interest in so-called primitive art, as well as to the work of contemporaries such as Alberto Giacometti. Like her colleagues, she adopted the view that art should primarily be concerned with psychic exploration and the mining of the personal subconscious. In 1982 Bourgeois published a photo-essay in *Artforum* in which she made public, for the first time, the disturbing scenario that had underpinned her privileged French childhood. She revealed that her father had, over a ten-year period, installed his mistress into the family home, radically undermining Bourgeois and her mother.[12] In the wake of this public revelation, Bourgeois increasingly concentrated on processes of psychological retrieval in her later work. Her 'cells' installations of the period 1991–94, for instance, dealt powerfully with a symbolic return to the scenes of early childhood. One of them, *Red Room (Child)*, was paired with another 'cell' titled *Red Room (Parents)* and clearly engaged with the conundrum of her psychic relationship with her parents. The two installations contained, along with a bed and other furnishings, numerous glass objects and spools. Bourgeois's family had been involved in the tapestry industry, and her mother, who had been a specialist restorer, was frequently symbolised by Bourgeois via spindle-like forms. In this instance, the sheer quantity of thread wound round the spools seemed to invoke a notion of unwinding, or unpicking the past (her mother had specialised in reuniting cut-up portions of tapestries via a process described by Bourgeois as '*rentrayage*: remake, reweave across the cut, rather like an invisible sewing'[13]). Around the time of the 'cells' Bourgeois had also begun to use other materials in her work which pointedly connoted the family business, namely fabrics, which in turn provided her practice with natural links to the attempts made by women since the 1960s to develop a specifically feminist mode of artistic production (via embroidery and so forth).

Looking at Bourgeois's *Oedipus*, which is one of the pieces which uses fabric, certain of the above biographical factors come into play, and coalesce with both the mythological and Freudian implications of Oedipus. In a vitrine we see ten small figures linked to the various episodes of the Oedipus myth: the Oracle (Janus-faced), Jocasta with Oedipus as a child, Oedipus as a baby with pinned legs, the murdered King Laius, the Sphinx, Oedipus sleeping with his mother Jocasta, Oedipus contemplating his fate, Oedipus's realization of his actions, Oedipus's blinding, and Oedipus being supported by his daughter Antigone. It cannot be coincidental that the figure of the elderly blinded Oedipus being led by his daughter has been related by art historians both to an early sculpture by Bourgeois, *The Blind Leading the Blind*, 1947–49, (which relates in turn to a photograph of Bourgeois's father leaning on her shoulder) and a large sculpture of Oedipus and Antigone which apparently stood at the foot of the staircase in the school attended by Bourgeois, the Lycée Fénelon.[14]

The interpretations that arise from this knowledge are open-ended; do the various riddles and blind actions, surrounding the central motif of incest, that constitute the Oedipus story, provide insight into the sense of dissembling that Bourgeois associated with her family background, and especially her father? Are we viewing here some playing-out of her own incestuous fantasies regarding her father, who is nevertheless punished heavily in the course of the imputed narrative, not least via his self-blinding at the recognition of his crimes? Images in the vitrine seem redolent of Bourgeois's obsessions in various ways; the image of Oedipus blinding himself can be associated with the fact that, in the myth, he supposedly put out his eyes with two pins from his dead mother's dress. This immediately returns us to the handicraft metaphors in Bourgeois output and her own associations with the idea of blindness ('I had to be blind to the mistress who lived with us. I had to be blind to the pain of my mother.'[15]).

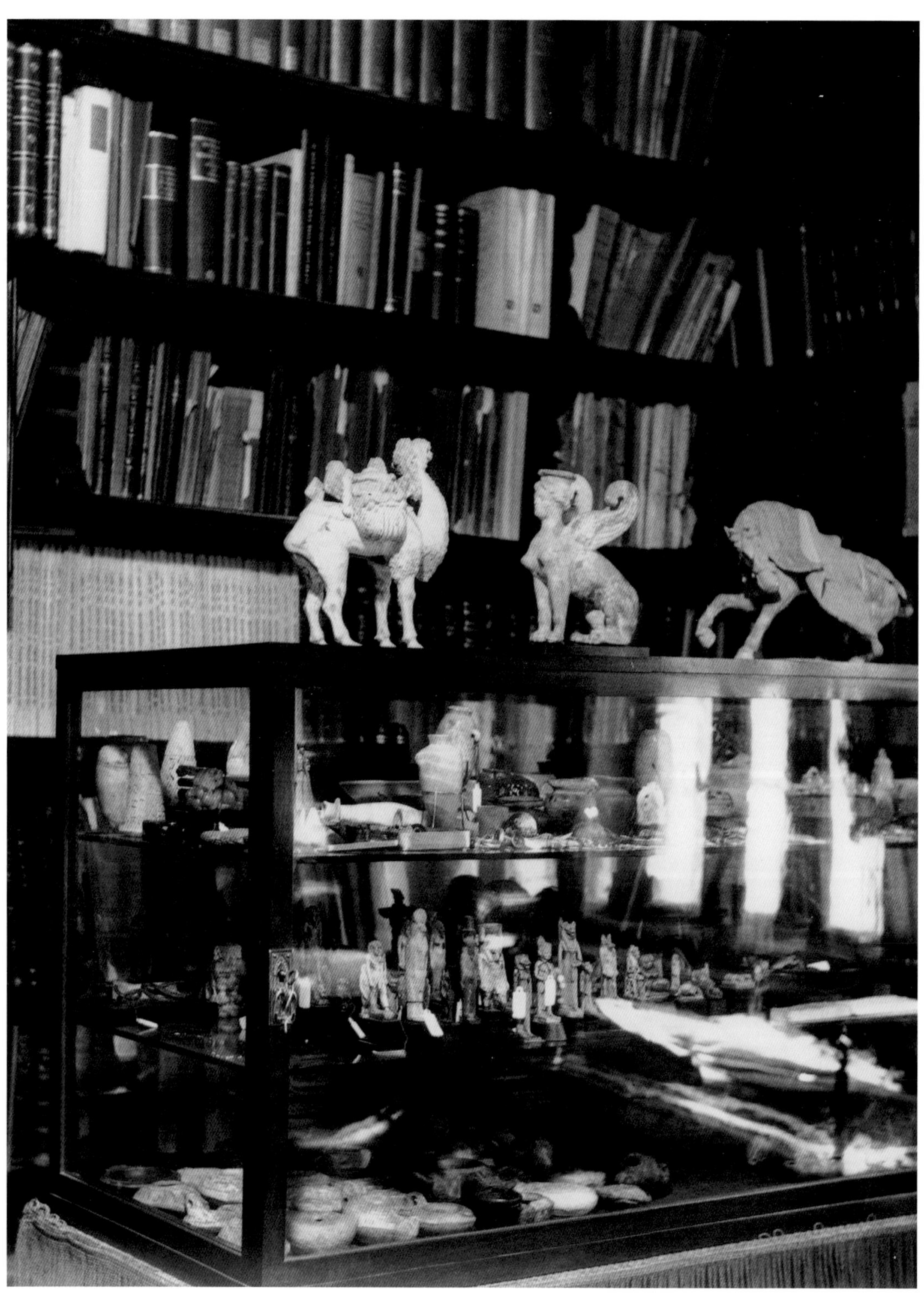

EDMUND ENGELMAN, *Freud's study*, 1938

Its psychological resonance is wide-reaching, but let us consider this vitrine more squarely in terms of this exhibition's theme, i.e. toys. In a sense Bourgeois's strategy in manufacturing these figures and configuring them in a symbolic matrix might be loosely related to the kind of play technique pioneered by the child psychologist Melanie Klein, who encouraged her child patients to use toys as emotional or symbolic counterparts.[16] (It is fascinating that, as Mignon Nixon notes, Bourgeois once considered becoming a child therapist.[17]) In a similar vein, the figurines have reminded Frances Morris of the 'crudely anatomical dolls a child victim-of-crime might be asked to use in a re-enactment of some trauma.'[18] More exactly attuned to their appearances, though, is Morris's observation that 'they seem like surrogates from a distant past, reminiscent in their fabrication of Peruvian grave dolls and of the swaddled bodies of Egyptian deities, safeguarding the past.'[19] This perception takes us back to a point made earlier; the difficulty that Ariès noted in distinguishing, historically speaking, between statuettes used in rituals and 'toys' in the modern sense of the word. Perhaps it is not surprising that Bourgeois herself explored the conjunction of the archaeological statuette and the toy in a text written in 1990 titled 'Freud's Toys.'[20]

Bourgeois's text was a review for an exhibition of Freud's personal collection of antiquities, and in it she ponders on the array of tiny Egyptian, Chinese, Greek and Roman figures with which Freud surrounded himself when writing. Seeing these as his 'toys,' Bourgeois is more sympathetic to them as tokens of his appetite for collecting than as objects which corresponded with his intellectual concerns. It is not difficult, though, to imagine the father of psychoanalysis meditating on these objects, which were displayed on his desktop and in several vitrines in his study, while he embarked on his archaeological probing of the human psyche. Bourgeois herself dismisses the idea as overly simplistic: 'the analogy is a cheap one. Anytime you are presented with a problem you dig ... we all dig for the truth. A cat will dig in the garden to hide its shit. We dig all day long, so the metaphor is obvious.'[21] Perhaps, however, she gave the analogy a second chance. Surely it is possible to see her returning to the idea of 'Freud's Toys,' some thirteen years after she had written the text, in the figurines of her own *Oedipus* vitrine.

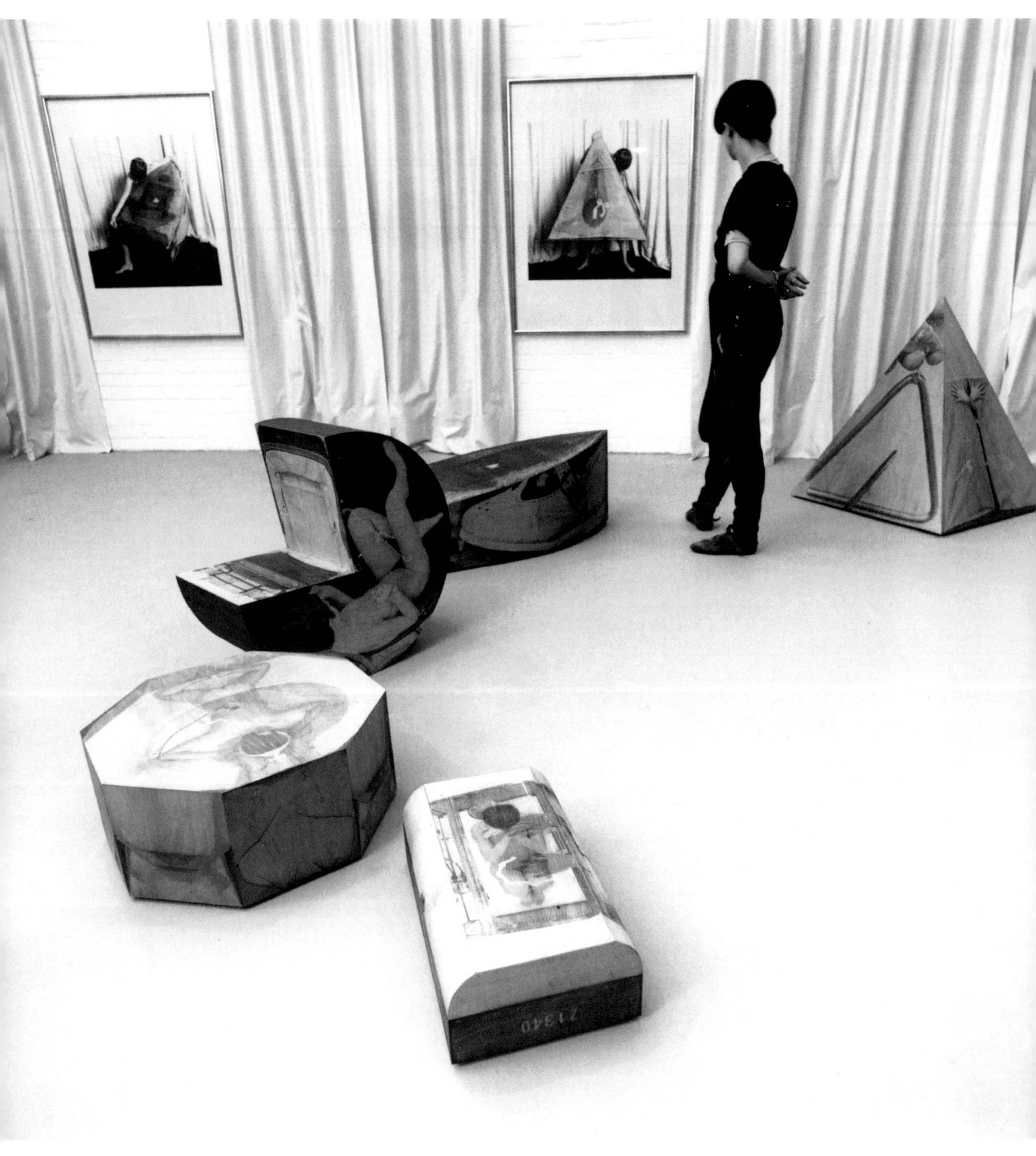

THE JUGGLER'S TABLE

However much Bourgeois's vitrine invites associations between toy-like figures and notions of archaeological/psychological retrieval, it also comments directly – as does the Oedipus myth – on the notion of destiny. In Bourgeois's miniaturised tableau the narrative that leads from the helpless infant in the mother's arms at the left, to the blind old man supported by his daughter at the right is laid out as though it were some pre-determined path punctuated by symbolically-significant encounters and events. Looking at these tiny mythic actors, our sense of poignancy is sparked, as it is in many myths, from a sense that humans are blind to the inexorability of their fates.

Bourgeois's preoccupation, as an ageing artist, with origins and destiny, can be correlated very interestingly with the work of a British artist, Helen Chadwick, (1953–96) who had produced a more obviously autobiographical narrative around twenty years earlier, in the form of her *Ego Geometria Sum*, which in its final version included a group of ten plywood objects printed with photographic imagery. Moving from one artist's work to the other, one is initially struck by massive differences. Scale is one of them: Bourgeois's figures are tiny whereas the wooden blocks that make up Chadwick's installation are keyed to the scale of the (growing) human body. Initially, Chadwick's work looks abstract in comparison with that of Bourgeois, but this is far from the case; closer examination reveals a profusion of imagery, some of it multiply superimposed via the photographic process (Chadwick used a photographic emulsion – Barfen's 'Silver Magic' which was then newly available). Both works have toy-like associations – of dolls/figurines in Bourgeois's case, as we have seen, and of a child's wooden blocks in the case of Chadwick. But the greatest similarity between them follows from their deployment of scattered configurations, ruled by a hidden logic.

opposite: HELEN CHADWICK photographed with *Ego Geometria Sum* at Riverside Studios, London, 1985
following pages: HELEN CHADWICK, *The Juggler's Table*, *c.* 1983

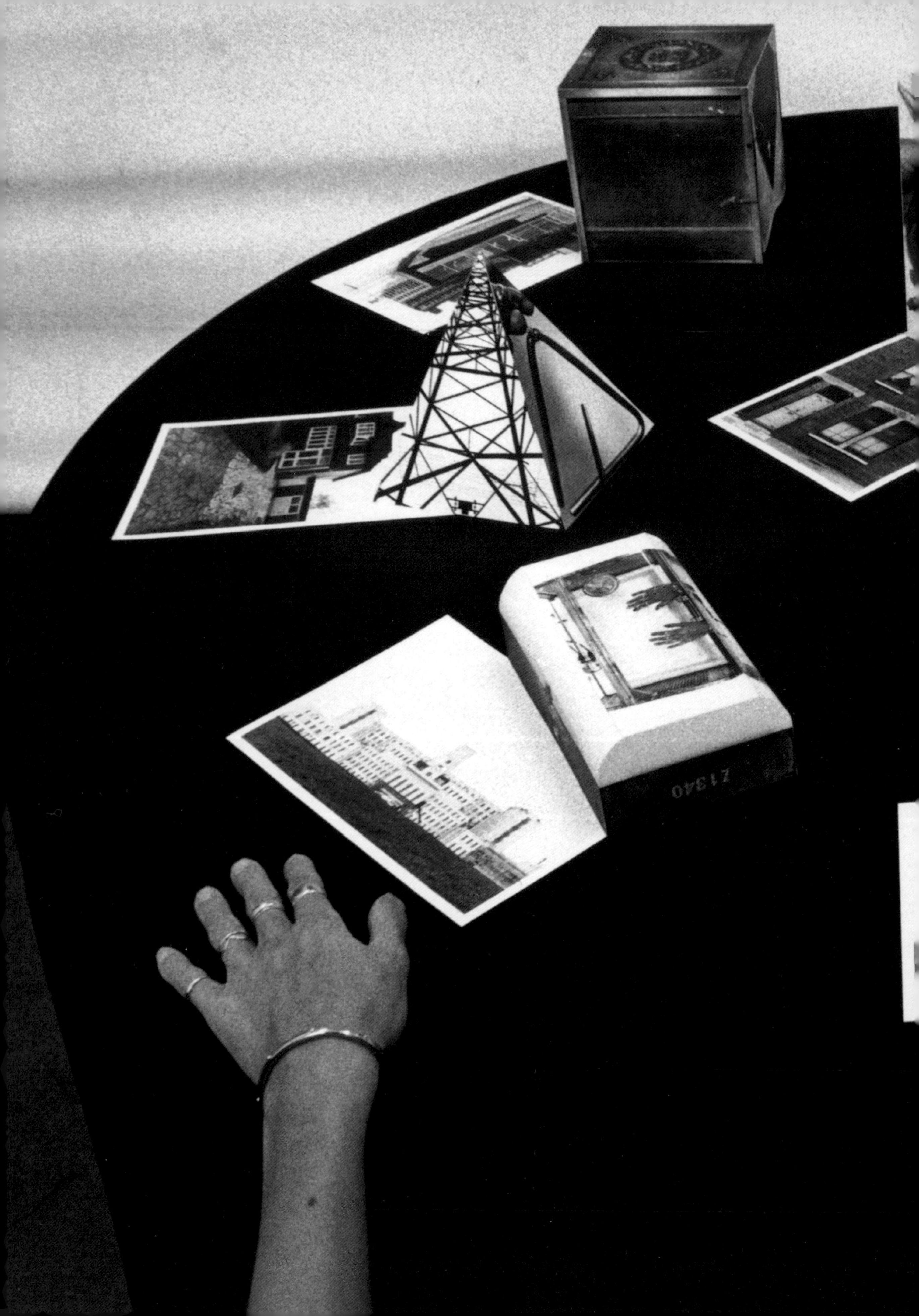
Z1340

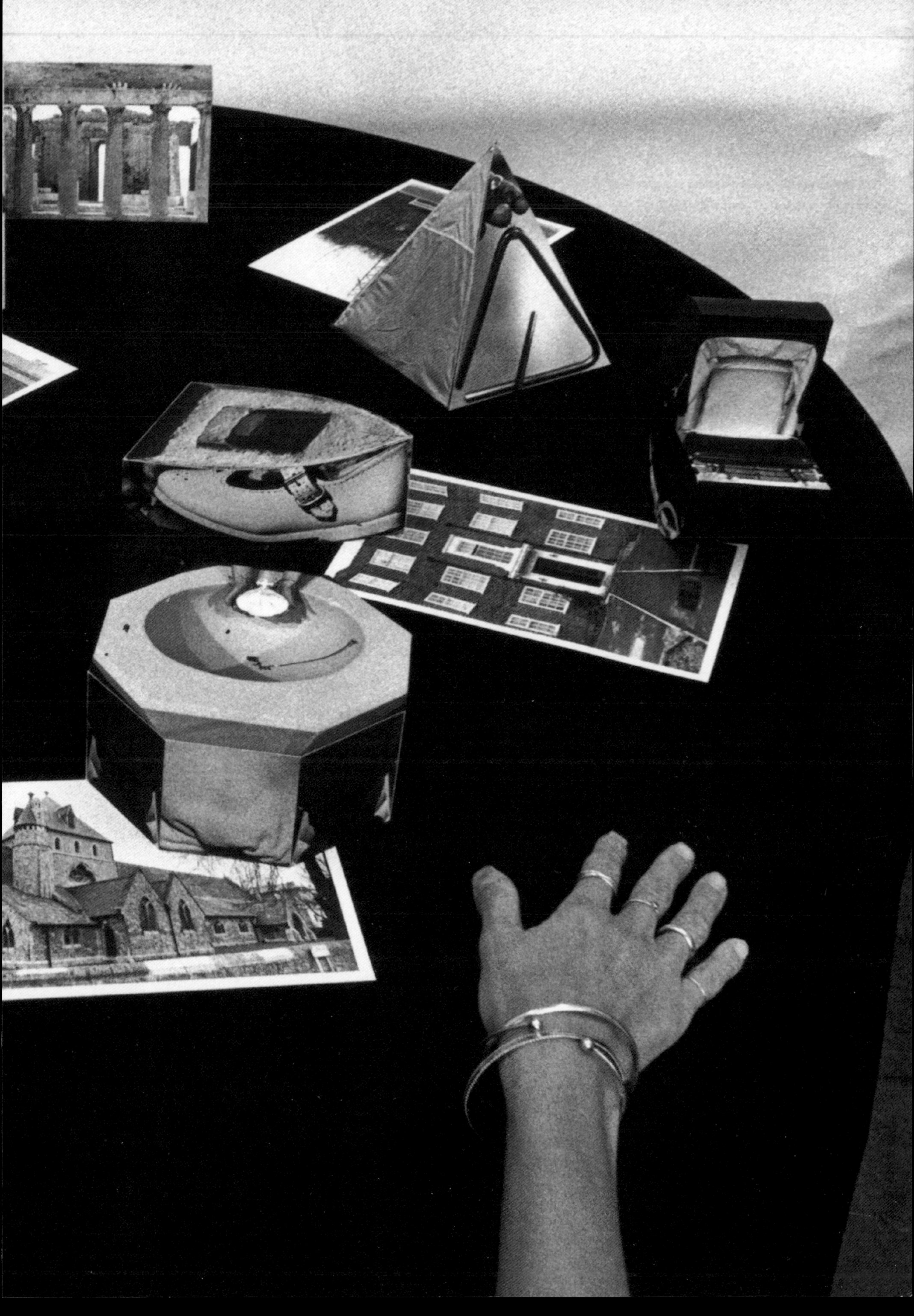

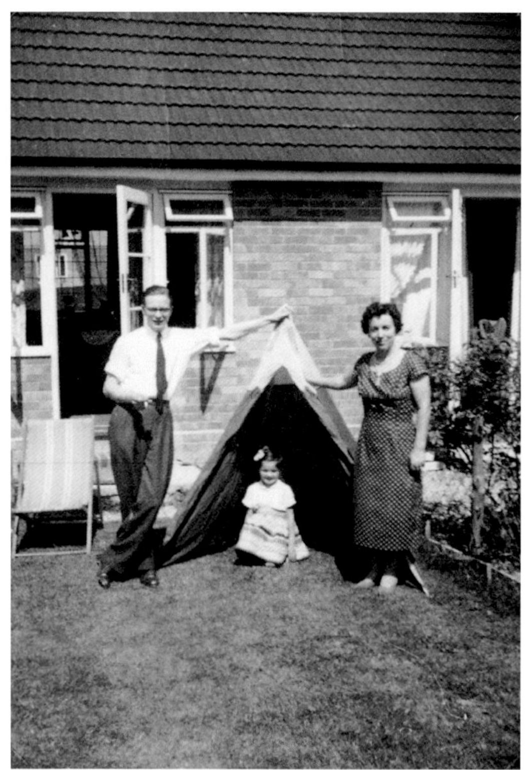

If, as already suggested, Bourgeois's cluster of miniature figures operates according to the unfolding of a mythic narrative, Chadwick's group of objects suggests the impression of a giant at play; as though her wooden objects have been haphazardly thrown onto the the gallery floor as part of some larger game. And given that, as we will see, each of these these blocks deal with some stage of Chadwick's early biographical development, one is inevitably drawn again into ideas of destiny or fate.

This aspect of Chadwick's installation is underlined when we consider how its individual pieces relate to *The Juggler's Table* (1983), which comprises a group of small maquettes, each a tiny cardboard model for the larger wooden equivalent, placed together on a table top with loose photographs of buildings which played a significant part in Chadwick's early life.

HELEN CHADWICK with her parents (undated), taken from the album, *Photographies*, compiled by Chadwick during her research for *Ego Geometria Sum*

Only occasionally exhibited as part of *Ego Geometria Sum* in the past, this piece, by its very title, suggests notions of the intervention of 'higher forces' in human destiny. One is particularly struck by the way in which the miniaturised nature of this arrangement reinforces the toy-like implication of the larger installation. (Indeed toys were among the fascinating items of memorabilia that Chadwick brought to bear on the larger finished objects, as is evident in Chadwick's photographic archives. One image, for instance shows a tiny Chadwick flanked by her parents in front of a scaled-down wigwam. Another bears the image of a troll with which she apparently identified on account of its short stature.[22])

The Juggler's Table is staged with its component parts placed on a round, black-draped table, reinforcing the idea that we are viewing the enigmatic contents of a child-entertainer's 'box of tricks'. (A further connotation is that of a fortune-teller, which is developed in certain photographs in which Chadwick's hands appear laid flat on the table-top, and in her notes for the project Chadwick recalled a 'Gypsy at Blackpool reading my hand'.[23]) Chadwick's early notes also indicate that Giorgio de Chirico's art and writings were at the back of her mind at this time, and more than anything one is reminded of a series of de Chirico's paintings of 1914–15, such as *The Evil Genius of a King*, which depicts toy-like objects on black table-like structures, which were foundational images for the surrealist understanding of the toy. De Chirico surely had these playthings in mind when he wrote about the 'enigma of the things generally considered insignificant':

> To live in a world as if in an immense museum of strangeness, full of curious many-coloured toys which change their appearance, which, like little children, we sometimes break to see how they are made on the inside, and, disappointed, realise they are empty.[24]

If de Chirico's toys place us in the position of interpreters of life's enigmas, Chadwick's objects on *The Juggler's Table* are similarly charged, although the allusion presumably is to the 'hand' one is dealt in life.

In discussing the sculptural objects of *Ego Geometria Sum*, Chadwick frequently emphasised that the relation between the geometrical regularity of each object and the anecdotal details of her life that are photographically registered on their surfaces derived from her concern with correlating microcosmic and macrocosmic phenomena, in the manner of the Pythagoreans.[25] Her overall strategy appears to have been a coming-to-terms with her past, motivated by a sense of self-alienation. Hence in a highly illuminating early note for the project she muses:

> Suppose one's body could be traced back through a succession of geometrical solids ... taking form from the pressure of recalled external forces ... the incubator, laundry-box, font, pram, boat, shoe, wigwam, bed, piano, desk, horse, temple, high school, door ... and if geometry is an expression of eternal and exact truths, inherent in the law of matter and thus manifestations of an absolute beauty, pre-destined ... then let this model of mathematical harmony be infused with a poetry of feeling and memory to sublimate the discord of past passion and desire in a recomposed neutrality of being.[26]

Chadwick only produced ten of these objects, which relate to her birth, infancy, childhood and adolescence up to age 30, which she observed is around the time the body stops growing.

GIORGIO DE CHIRICO, *The Evil Genius of a King*, 1914–15

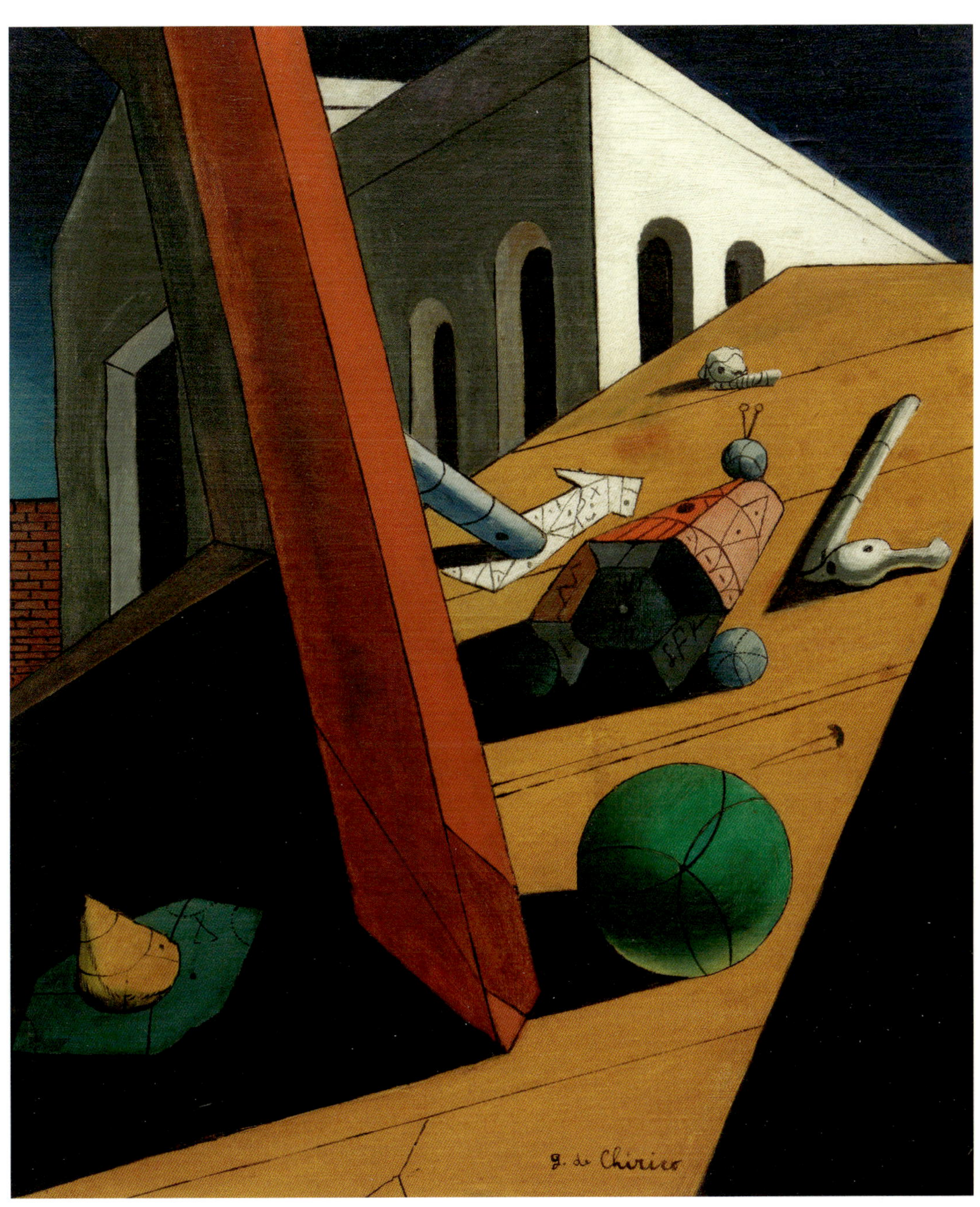
g. de Chirico

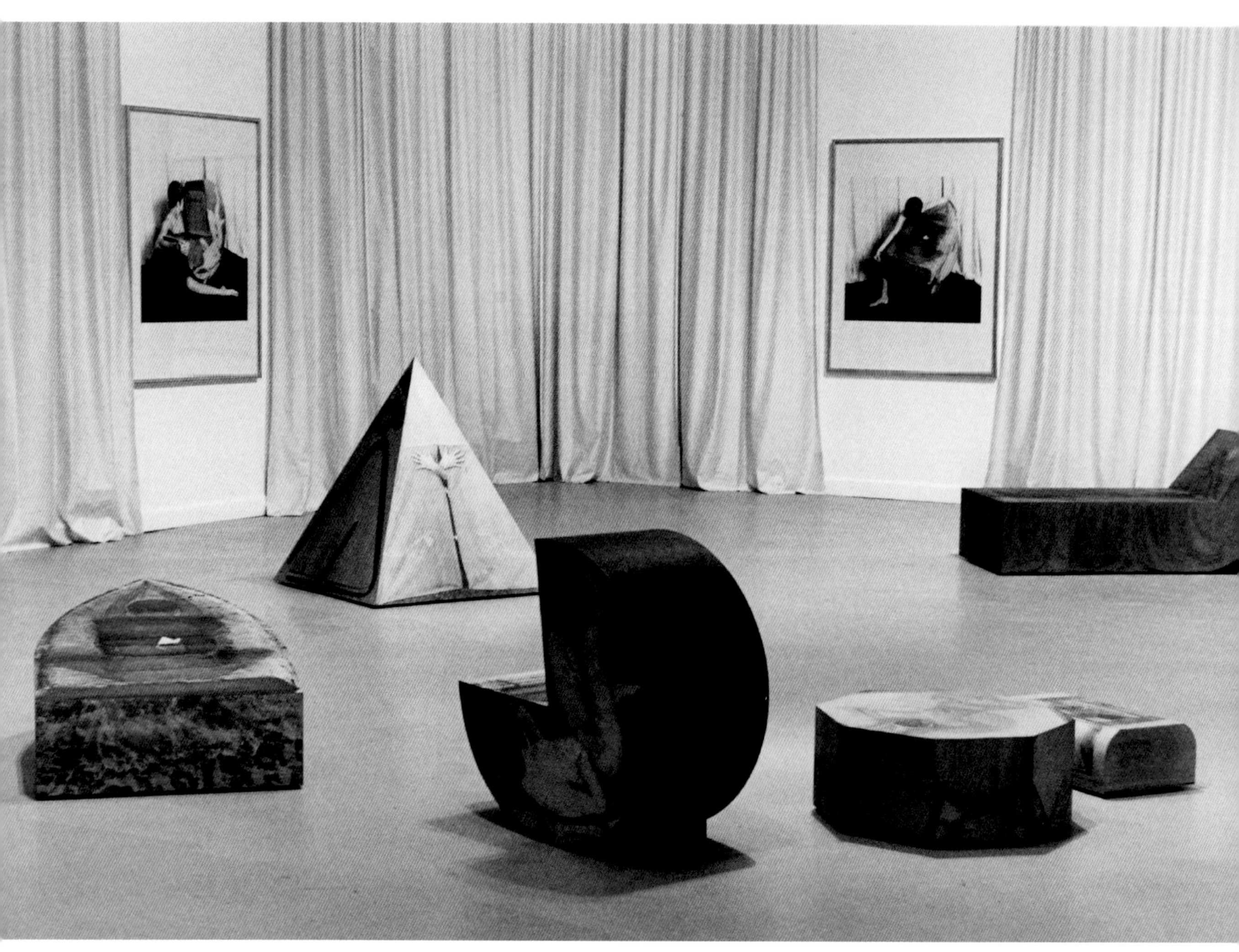

These comprise *Incubator, birth; Font, aged 3 months; Pram, aged 10 months; Boat, aged 3 years; Wigwam, aged 5 years; Bed, aged 6 3/4 years; Piano, aged 9 years; Horse, aged 11 years; High School, aged 13 years; Statue, aged 15–30 years* and the decision has been made in this exhibition to show five of them referring to infancy and childhood. In her notes for the project Chadwick returned again and again to the ghostly effects produced by printing with photographic emulsion on plywood and spoke of a desire to 'lay my ghosts', noting, elliptically, at one point: 'ghost appears lost in time cut through image'.[27] She seems to have understood the printed facets of the objects as slices cut through time, by means of which she was able to re-inhabit the past, and there is a weird sense in which the adult images of Chadwick imprinted onto the objects revisit (or haunt) the sites of her younger self's activities. At the same time, the adult Chadwick re-enacts the actions of her child-self, heroically attempting to adjust herself to the shape of the object concerned whilst simultaneously combating the sense in which the solid object appears to entrap her (a further note for the project, eerily looking forward rather than backwards, speculates on a coffin as one of the geometrical objects: 'penultimate object = coffin body truly within it.'[28]) There is, thus, a strong sense in which, through these ghostly images, Chadwick replays the reining-in of the child's instinct for play and exploration by a set of social hurdles and expectations; a process of unavoidable socialisation.

Chadwick's wooden objects speak of her transition through the various phases of childhood, retrieved through the most exacting discipline of *remembering*, as well her most intimate negotiations with mute and obdurate things. Sometimes an element of play predominates. *Boat, aged 3 years*, for instance, takes its entire form from a large sandcastle specially made by the artist for the project. On one of its sides, there is an image of the artist's arm and hand reaching out to plant a miniature flag in a sandcastle, a homage to British seaside culture. But more often, the objects have a darker edge. The pyramidal *Wigwam, aged 5 years* seems especially telling in this respect. Based on the

opposite: HELEN CHADWICK, installation photograph of *Ego Geometria Sum* at the Venice Biennale, 1984

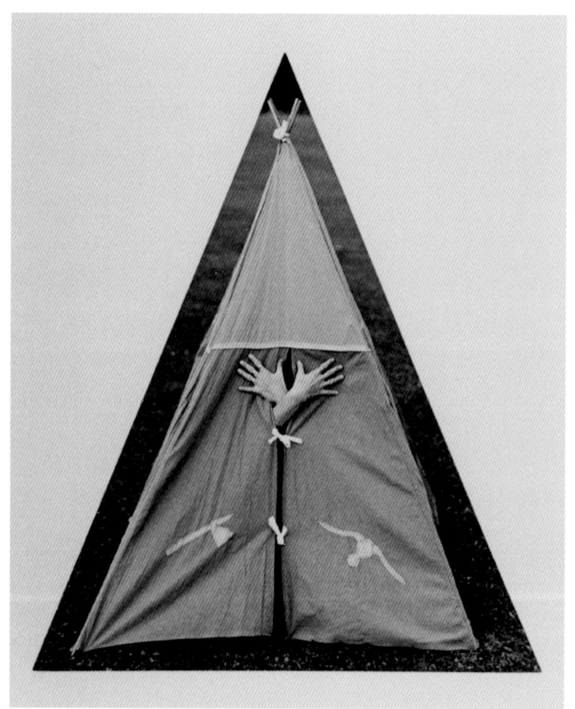

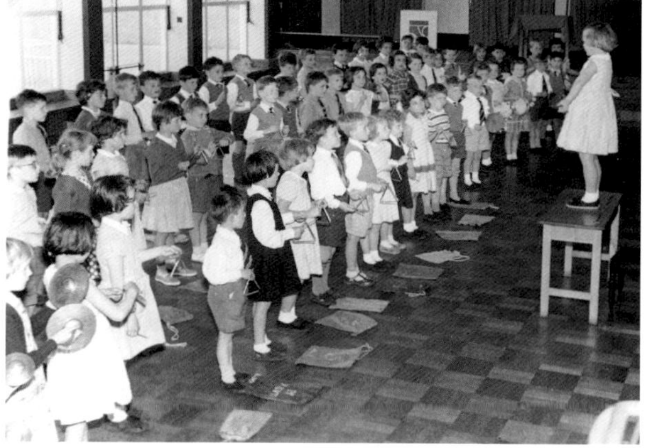

family photograph of Chadwick posing before a tent, the object is covered with images that suggest entrapment with, on one facet, two splayed hands emerging, half-jokingly, half-sinisterly, from the closed tent flap, and, on another facet, the rhyming shape of a triangle; an instrument played by Chadwick at school, and thus evocative of the socially-prescribed imperative to be able to play an instrument. If, as has been suggested, the relation of objects such as this to their tiny maquettes on *The Juggler's Table* indicates that the sculptures are, at a certain level, play-blocks – not so much of a child but of some abstract principle of destiny – then these toys end up being tokens of control as much as freedom. But this is, of course, what toys often are.

HELEN CHADWICK
left: photograph of a wigwam and the artist's hands (undated). This image appears on *Ego Geometria Sum: The Wigwam, aged 5 years*, 1983
right: photograph of children playing the triangle taken from the album, *Photographies*, compiled by Chadwick during her research for *Ego Geometria Sum*

NOTES

11. Jacques Derrida, 'Structure, Sign, and Play', in his *Writing and Difference*, (trans. Alan Bass), Routledge & Kegan Paul, London, 1978, reprinted 1990, p. 280.
12. Louise Bourgeois, 'Child Abuse', *Artforum*, vol. 20, no. 4, December 1982, pp. 40–47.
13. Louise Bourgeois, 'A Memoir: Louise Bourgeois and Patricia Beckert', in *Destruction of the Father / Reconstruction of the Father: Writings and Interviews 1923–1997*, Violette Editions, London, 1998, p. 121.
14. Marie-Laure Bernadac, *Louise Bourgeois*, Flammarion, Paris, 2006, p. 168.
15. Louise Bourgeois, 'The Passion for Sculpture: A Conversation with Alain Kirili', in *Destruction of the Father / Reconstruction of the Father*, op. cit., p. 179.
16. Juliet Mitchell (ed.), *The Selected Melanie Klein*, Peregrine Books, Harmondsworth, 1986.
17. Mignon Nixon, 'Psychoanalysis: Louise Bourgeois Reconstructing the Past, in Frances Morris (ed.), *Louise Bourgeois*, Tate Publishing, London, 2007, p. 233.
18. Frances Morris, 'Louise Bourgeois: Stitches in Time' in *Stitches in Time* (exh. cat.), August Projects, London and IMMA, Dublin, 2003, p. 30.
19. Ibid.
20. Louise Bourgeois, 'Freud's Toys', reprinted in *Destruction of the Father / Reconstruction of the Father*, op. cit., pp. 186–190.
21. Ibid., p. 187.
22. 'My Personal Museum', *Ego Geometria Sum: From the Helen Chadwick Archive* (exhibition leaflet), Henry Moore Institute, Leeds, 2004.
23. Helen Chadwick's notebook, Helen Chadwick Archive, Henry Moore Institute, Leeds.
24. Giorgio de Chirico, *Il meccanismo del pensiero. Critica, polemica, autobiografia 1911–1943*, Turin, 1985, p. 18.
25. For Chadwick's interest in Pythagoras, via Arthur Koestler's *The Sleepwalkers*, 1959, see Eva Martischnig, 'Getting Inside the Artist's Head', in Mark Sladen (ed.), *Helen Chadwick* (exh. cat.), Barbican Art Gallery, London and Hatje Cantz, Ostfildern, 2004, p. 51.
26. Helen Chadwick, *Enfleshings*, Secker and Warburg, London, 1989, p. 9.
27. Helen Chadwick's notebook, Helen Chadwick Archive, Henry Moore Institute, Leeds.
28. Ibid.

CHAPTER 2

INSIDE THE PLAYROOM

ROBERT GOBER
AND JEFF KOONS

Much of the most emblematic art of the 1980s and 1990s in Britain and the US – especially that which dovetails most easily with ideas of postmodernism – deals with the theme of the commodity or with the way in which the mass media has become increasingly invasive. The concern with origins and with the psycho-biographical that is evident in the work of Louise Bourgeois and Helen Chadwick might, on the face of it, seem far removed from such dominant trends. At a time when the artist was seen by many, not so much as the fount of originality, but instead as someone who shuffles existing social and cultural codes, and in which the most challenging art often eschewed artistic self-revelation in favour of the re-presentation of the copy or the simulacrum, the interests of Bourgeois and Chadwick may seem anachronistic – out of kilter with the zeitgeist.[29] In this respect, it is interesting to turn to two major US artists, Robert Gober and Jeff Koons, whose work sits more comfortably with such accounts of the period and to approach their work from a different vantage point through the subject of toys and childhood.

PLAYPEN

In the early 1980s, the work that Gober was producing – sculptures taking the form of weirdly dysfunctional sinks and urinals – were occasionally exhibited alongside signature works by Koons such as *New Hoover Convertible* (1980), his plexiglass-encased vacuum cleaner. At that time such sculptural pieces, together with those of a number of other New York-based artists such as Ashley Bickerton, Haim Steinbach and Meyer Vaisman, were seen as participating in a general trend toward 'appropriation' in which issues of authenticity – the relationship of the object to its original model (which was usually a utilitarian object and part of commodity culture – were at issue). In time, it became apparent that Gober's work was different in its concerns from the appropriationists, but, given his allusions, in his urinals in particular, to the father of the readymade, Marcel Duchamp, who in turn was an evident influence on Koons, it seemed fitting to many critics to bring these artists together.

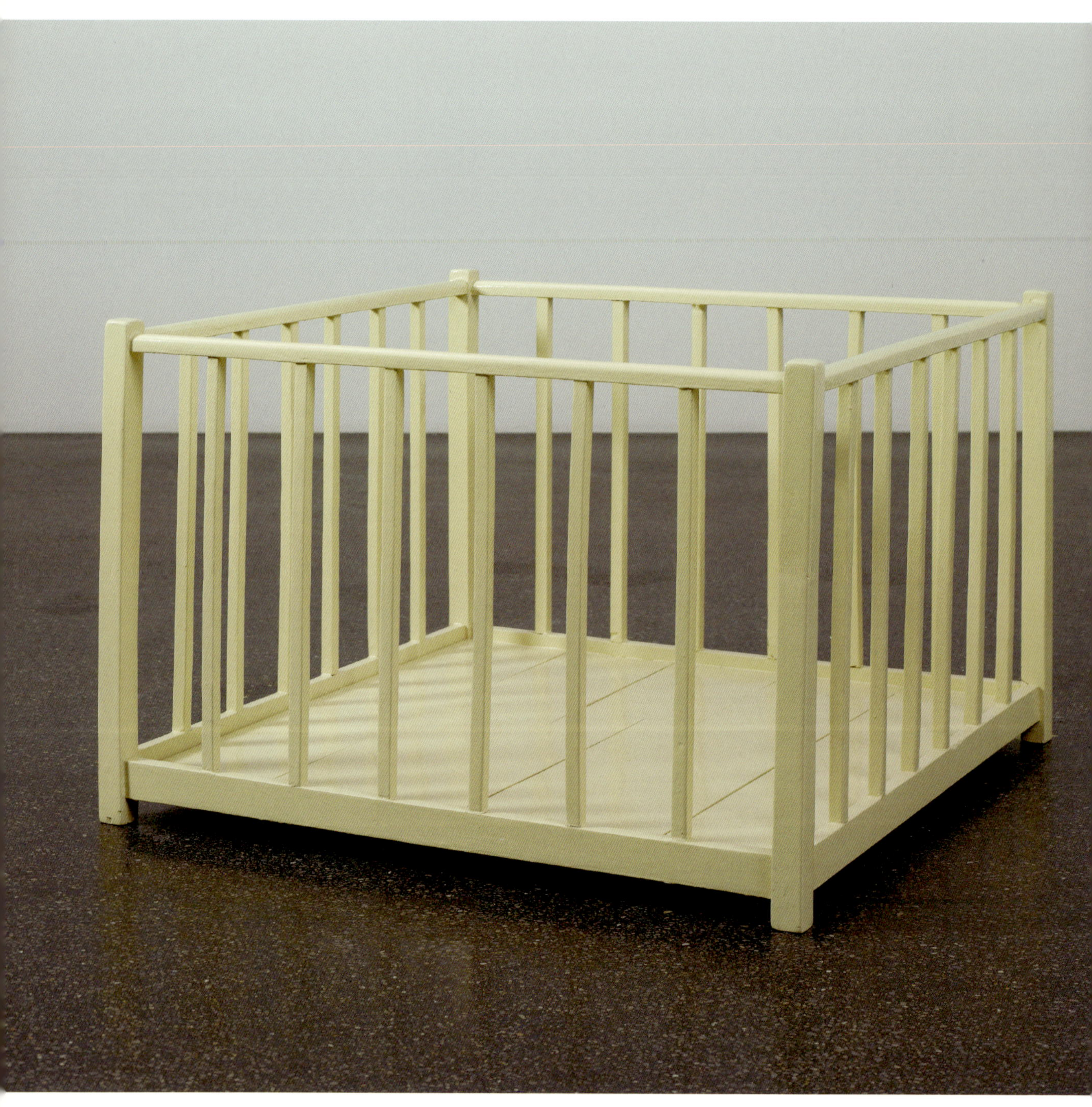

The truth was that Gober's work was far removed from the principle of the readymade. Like Jasper Johns before him, Gober took objects from everyday life and re-made them with an enormous degree of respect for craftsmanship and for the process of making. (Something similar might later be said of Koons, but at this early stage his practice was aligned more closely with the anti-aesthetic principle of the readymade). In fact, it was on thematic grounds that Koons and Gober had most in common. As Joan Simon notes, the work of Gober and Koons – like certain others of their generation who were responding to the concurrence of the AIDS crisis and the fragile affluence of mid-1980s America – could be seen as returning, however ironically, to 'the safe haven of home', and looking back to their childhoods in the 1950s (Gober was born in 1954, Koons in 1955).[30]

As commentators on Gober have frequently stated, his turn to domestic themes in the mid-1980s was anything but straightforwardly nostalgic or reassuring. In the mid-1980s he produced an extensive series of sculptures of beds, cribs and playpens which were modelled on objects from the time of his childhood. That they are very much period pieces is important to stress; in some of the playpens, for instance, the edges of the wooden boards that make up the base are visible beneath their covering of paint giving a home-made feel which is quite different from the streamlined look one might find in products of the 1980s. Such objects – and *Playpen* of 1986 is an excellent example – seem in their rather drab, colourless appearance to reflect the austerity of the 1950s. In this respect they pointedly engage in dialogue with the times in which they were produced – the affluent 1980s. (It should also be noted that these objects reference the minimalist sculpture by Donald Judd and Sol LeWitt that Gober grew up with as an art student; they therefore take in a complex personal/artistic genesis.)

The objects, of course, obliquely comment on attitudes to parenting in the 1950s. There is a sense in which the playpen, far from representing play and freedom, is in fact a figuring of domestic containment or even imprisonment; it is a cage in which to enclose the child as much as a site of pleasure. The very absence of toys from the place in which they might be expected to be found reinforces this slightly chilling impression. Despite belonging to the era of Dr Spock (whose 1946

ROBERT GOBER, *Burnt House*, 1980

book *The Common Sense of Baby and Child Care* offered 1950s parents a newly liberal attitude to childcare), one senses that these works speak of a more emotionally buttoned-up era, and Gober has alluded quite extensively in later works to his strict Catholic upbringing.[31] This concern with the way the child's agency is constrained by the very domestic items designed to support its development sets up a particular resonance with Chadwick, also a child of the 1950s.

To dwell briefly on the theme of toys in Gober's output, it is interesting to note that he had produced several dollhouse sculptures in the early 1980s. While these raise fascinating questions about gender stereotypes in relation to toys and the development of children's sexuality (if one relates this to Gober's identity as a gay artist), they also function as repositories for disturbing memories. In connection with his *Burnt House* (1980), Gober has recollected that: 'When I was young ... a house across the street from us was engulfed in flames. A mother and her son were outside the house and the mother was hysterical because her youngest child was inside.'[32] One becomes aware, therefore, that even the most innocuous childhood-related objects in Gober's art can be redolent of trauma.

Gober's domestic objects that are more obviously related to trauma – his distorted cribs for example – have led critics like Hal Foster to employ a psychoanalytically-loaded lexicon of the uncanny and the abject to describe Gober's practice, but it is arguably the artist's straight replicas of his domestic past which convey the most through their muteness. Gober has said, 'I always try to get people to focus less ... on finding "meaning" ... in the work, but to focus on what it is exactly, what it is physically made of and how it is made. A lot of times metaphors are almost embedded in the medium.'[33] In this respect the critic Dave Hickey makes the extremely telling point that Gober's re-making may in fact be seen as a subtle queering of 'the real' in line with a fundamentally homosexual apprehension of the world: 'there is latent in the world a whole "Other" construction of "nature" and what is "natural" – an Other reality coextensive with the Euclidean hegemony of heterosexual culture but *prior* to it, and eternally out of phase with it.'[34] Taking this view, Gober's replication of objects from his childhood should be read as the means by which he recapitulates

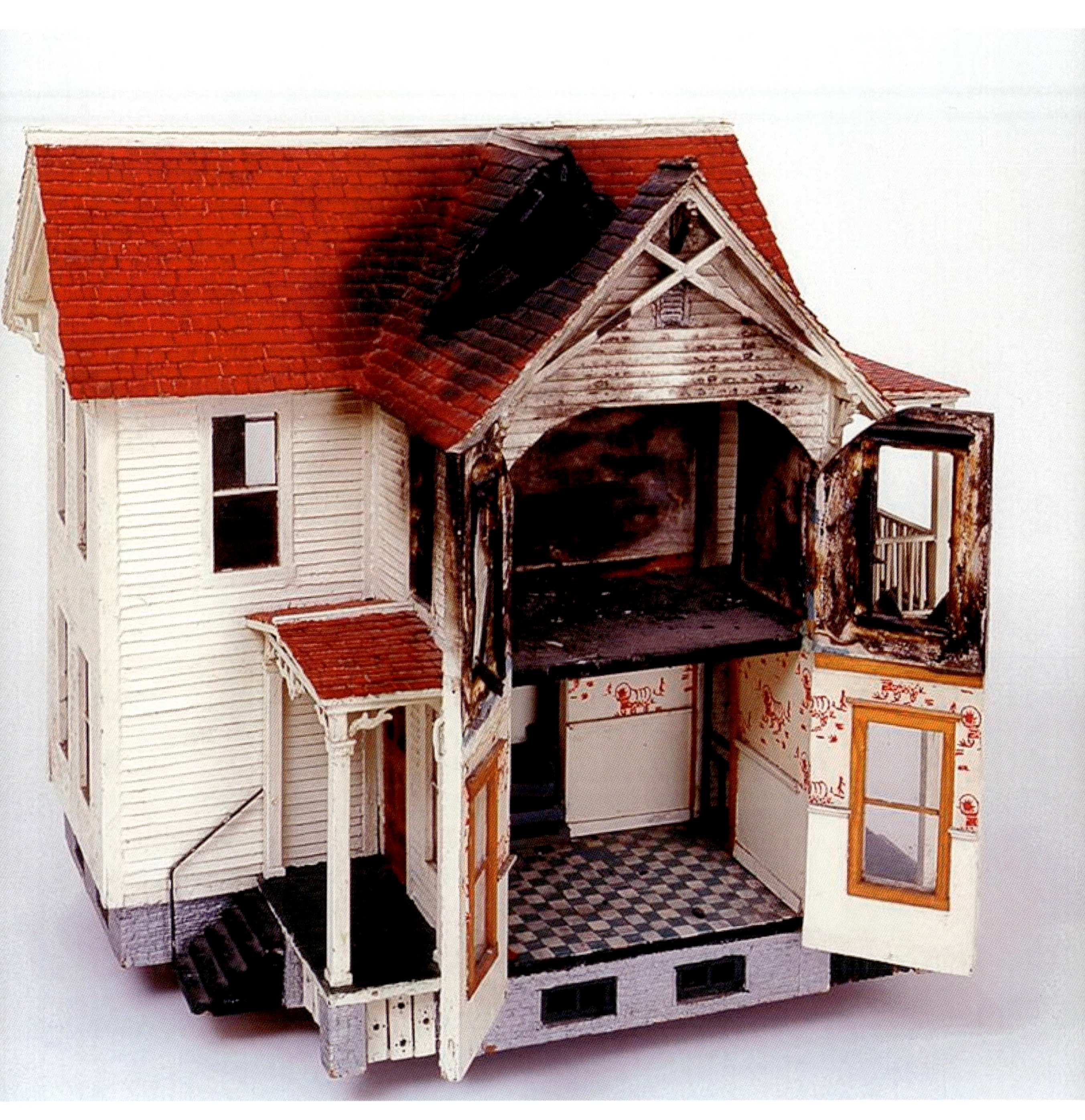

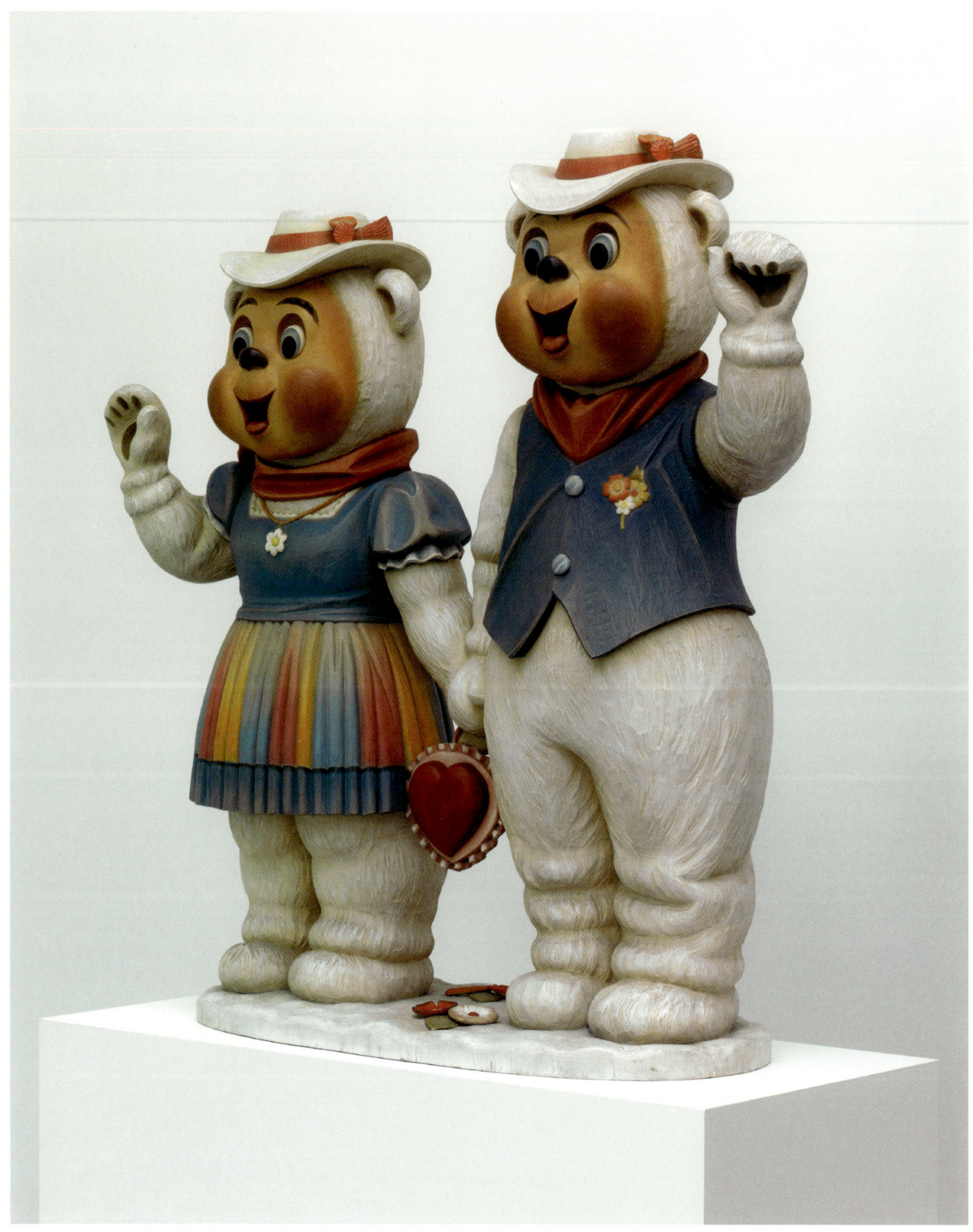

JEFF KOONS, *Winter Bears*, 1988

the emergence of his sexuality against models of so-called normalcy. One aspect of his re-creation of past objects is especially poignant in relation to precisely the material in which his playpens were fabricated – wood. The critic Elisabeth Sussman has made the shrewd point that 'the sources of Gober's early sculptures share the particular everydayness of the period, the last moment in America before plastic was a common manufacturing material'.[35] Gober's return to wood, at a time when plastics were more the order of the day, seems bound up with a remaking of the past which does indeed have the connotation of physical making (i.e. craftsmanship) built into it.

BEARS

Roland Barthes' essay, 'Toys', of 1957, contains a passionate defence of wood as a material for the making of playthings, in opposition to the increasing use of plastics in manufacturing:

> Current toys are made of graceless material, the product of chemistry, not of nature. Many are now moulded from complicated mixtures; the plastic material of which they are made ... destroys all the pleasure, the sweetness, the humanity of touch. A sign which fills one with consternation is the gradual disappearance of wood, in spite of its being an ideal material because of its firmness and softness ... Wood removes, from all the forms which it supports, the wounding quality of angles which are too sharp, the chemical coldness of metal ... It is a familiar and poetic substance which does not sever the child from close contact with the tree, the table, the floor.[36]

This nostalgia for wood (which for Barthes was an anti-bourgeois stance but now seems thoroughly bourgeois in its connotations) may well be correlated ironically with Gober's re-creation of 1950s nursery furnishings (bearing in mind that Gober re-works the past without necessarily feeling nostalgic about it). It is even more fascinating, however, to consider Barthes' diatribe in relation to

Jeff Koons, the artist of the 1980s and 1990s who is most readily associated with the kind of brightly-coloured, kitschy toys – products of mass culture and the advertising industry – that Barthes would most readily have despised.

Koons, of course, has been a highly visible figure in international art since the string of exhibitions in the 1980s that made his name: 'The New' (1980), 'Equilibrium' (1985), 'Luxury and Degradation' (1986), and *Banality* (1988–89). From the beginning critics often responded negatively to his apparently tongue-in-cheek valorisation of commodity culture. His fellow artist, Sherrie Levine, described him as possessing 'all the ingratiating enthusiasm of a quiz show host whose prizes reveal an extraordinary consistency beneath their apparent variety. Intoxication is their theme: intoxication with the effects of novelty, alcohol, money and possession.'[37] Koons's subject matter in the early exhibitions was in fact partly lifted from the mass media (with references to the Pink Panther or Michael Jackson for instance), and partly from the array of imagery found in gift shops, television and magazines, but with aspects of the colour, scale, composition and detail of the original sources carefully altered. While Koons had used the Duchampian strategy of the readymade earlier in his career, by the time of the *Banality* series in the late 1980s he was hiring craftsmen to produce his objects for him. The materials were far removed from the plastics so abhorrent to Barthes; while certain objects in this exhibition were made of porcelain, a number of them made use of polychromed wood (such as *Buster Keaton*, (1988, a five-foot-tall sculpture of the comic actor astride a donkey, or *String of Puppies*, 1988); chiming with precisely the note of nostalgia that Barthes had sounded.

Two of the most important polychromed wood pieces from the *Banality* series, *Winter Bears* (1988) and *Bear and Policeman* (1988), are included in 'Childish Things'. Thinking about the series' concentration on toys or playthings, it would be wrong to consider these pieces as relating

JEFF KOONS, *Bear and Policeman*, 1988

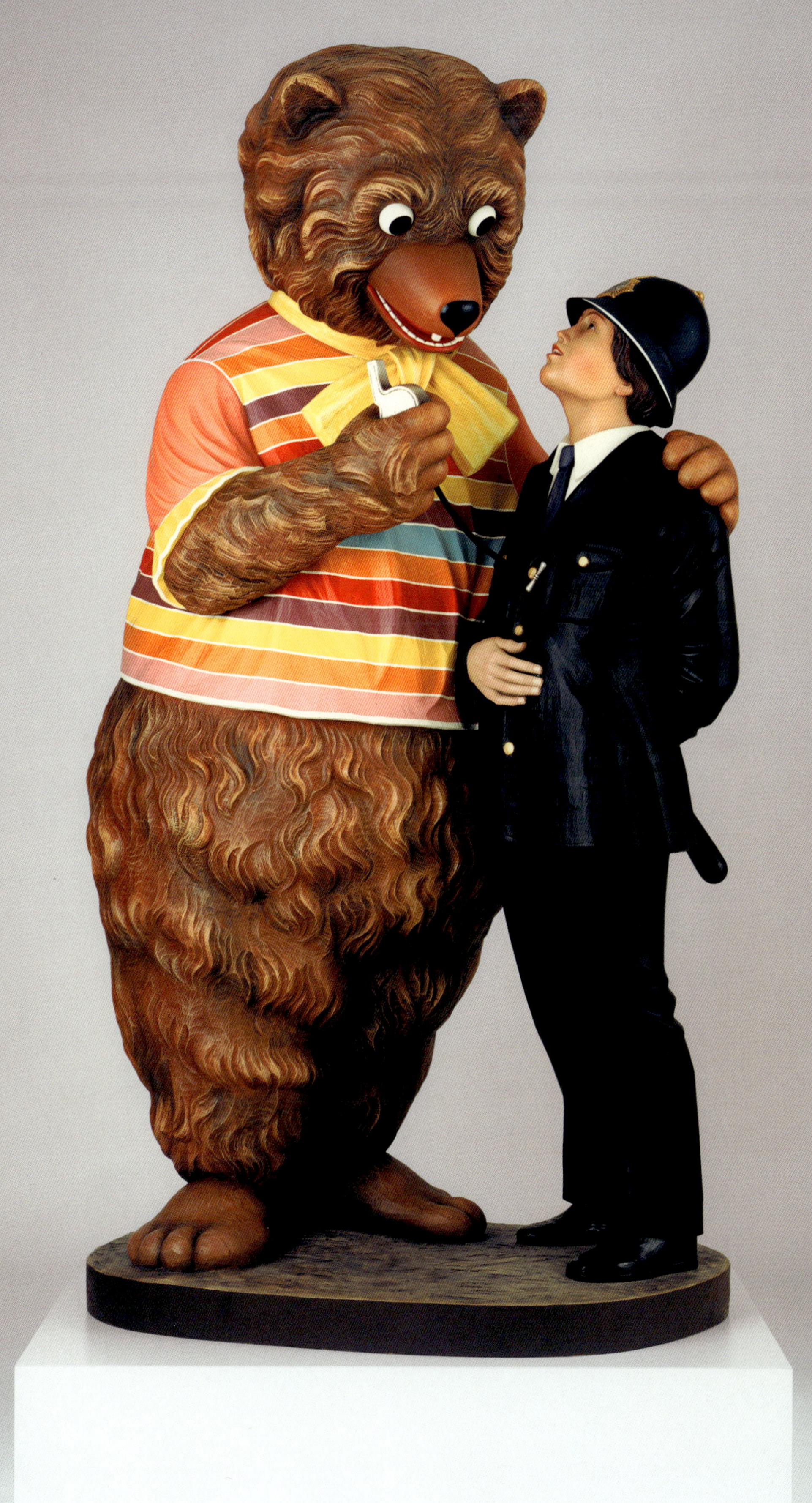

straightforwardly to such a category; they are clearly massively enlarged versions of ornaments or knick-knacks that might be found in a child's bedroom – objects of consolation, fantasy or amusement, rather than things that can be actively played with (although they might well be handled and caressed). But a deep nostalgia for the iconography of childhood is undoubtedly attached to them, and this can be indexed to Koons's own childhood, which is a source for much of his work. This backward-looking impulse, in which the use of wood implicitly suggests an ambivalence towards shifts in manufacturing that occurred between the 1950s and the 1980s, helps to reinforce the generational affinities that link Koons and Gober, although Koons's reversion to the past appears more blithe and less bound up with malaise than Gober's.

However, a close consideration of the two works by Koons which were selected for 'Childish Things', suggests a slightly more sinister reading. Critics have often pointed to the darkness lurking behind Koons's saccharine visions. Kirk Varnedoe and Adam Gopnik, writing in the catalogue for New York's Museum of Modern Art's 'High & Low: Modern Art and Popular Culture' exhibition of 1991, saw Koons's 1980s figurines as, '... nightmarish – devil dolls, in which the insipid language of the cartoons' over accentuated contours and biscuit glazes was suddenly made hard and staring. The contours of each piece were as chubby as a Disney drawing, glacially hard – like Muppets who had just seen the Medusa.'[38] Stuart Morgan noted the manic quality of the *Winter Bears* who 'waving and smiling' present an image of madness.'[39] And Koons himself talked rather enigmatically of sexual harassment in relation to his *Bear and Policeman*: 'In *Bear and Policeman* it is a man who is being sexually toyed with. That was to show banality out of control, and that you can have somebody come along and exploit power.'[40]

The image of the enormous bear infantilising the policeman, the adult figure of authority, and interfering with him by removing his whistle, represents, of course, a reversal of the traditional power relations between humans and bears emblematised, for instance, by the familiar image of a man leading a dancing or performing bear by a leash. One is reminded of the fact that, beyond the tourist souvenir associations of this particular object (the policeman is an archetypal 'London bobby' from the 1960s and 1970s and would have held a certain exotic charm for an American child), bears are deeply embedded in the folk consciousness of mankind. As 'the beast that walks like men' they have been both feared and adored through the centuries, as reflected in fairy tales such as *Goldilocks and the Three Bears*. In his history of the relationship between people and bears, Bernd Brunner notes that the popularity of the teddy bear in modern times derives from the affinity that exists between the features of bears' faces and those of children: 'the generalized representation of a diminutive, toothless bear with a snub nose, fat cheeks ... and a cuddly body beneath its fur possess all the traits that awaken sympathy in humans and motivate them to buy.'[41] At a time in America when a wave of nostalgia for teddy bears, and a marked surge in their manufacture, was taking place (see also Haim Steinbach's *basics* (1986; p. 64) and Mike Kelley's *Arena #7 (Bears)* (1990; p. 61), Koons returns us to the darker connotations of these cultural symbols.[42] In spite of Koons's apparent identification with all that is new and brash, there is a folkloric subtext to such pieces. This is reinforced by the scale of *Bear and Policeman* – its gigantism. The critic Susan Stewart sees the image of the giant as 'linked to the earth in its most primitive, or natural, state' and hence as a 'violator of boundary and rule'. Koons's exploitation of scale here, for all its Pop art links to Claes Oldenburg or to the genial giants of Disney World, has precisely this primordial undertow.[43]

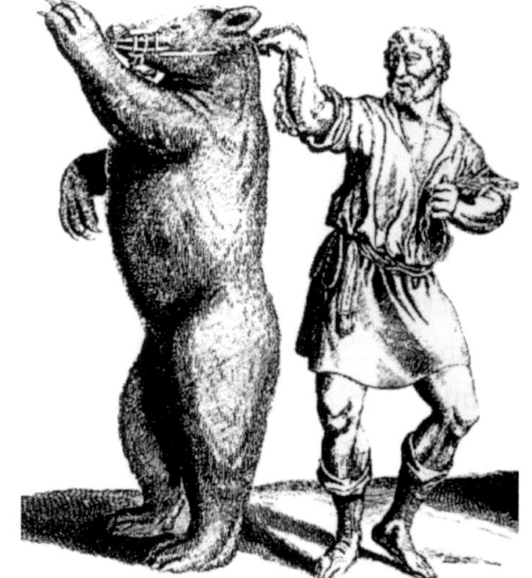

Illustration of a bear and his Roman master from Bernd Brunner's *Bears: A Brief History*, Yale University Press, 2007

More than anything, though, it is Koons's use of wood that consolidates the folkloric association. In this respect his sculptures of bears might be seen as drawing on handicraft traditions, particularly German ones, in which carved bears were prominent.[44] Whilst working on his bears, along with other pieces, for the *Banality* exhibition, Koons spent time in Munich and seems also to have been influenced by the Rococo and Counter-Reformation woodcarvings that he found in local churches. He himself said: 'When I work with wood it is so people can feel the security of religion.'[45] Talking more generally about 'Banality', he also asserted that the exhibition was 'about communicating to the bourgeois class. I wanted to remove their guilt and shame about the banality that motivates them and which they respond to.'[46] His antidote to their malaise was an extra-strong dose of the kitsch they claimed to find unpalatable. But this was served up, as we have seen, with comforting helpings of folklore and religion.

To return to Barthes' crusade for wooden toys, it is evident that Koons can be seen as taking up the critic's cause in his bear pieces, although highly ironically. Koons knew, full well, that it was a bourgeois nostalgia for childish things, for the disappearing wooden toys and ornaments of the mid-1950s playroom, to which he was appealing, and this was a nostalgia that he himself partly shared. He was perfectly capable, in his toy-related works of the 1980s, of a more hard-nosed celebration of the glitzy and the ultra-modern – his most emblematic work, the shiny *Rabbit* of 1986 (p. 9), bears this out. By the late 1990s Koons was producing more straightforwardly celebratory re-creations of kiddie-kitsch such as his *Balloon Dog (Blue) (*1994–2000) which clearly fetishise the industrial materials of late-twentieth-century toy manufacture rather than wood. But however much such works project a love of the shallow and the frivolous, we can see the metaphysical edge to his iconography of childhood and play in these wooden bear sculptures of the late 1980s. This talk of metaphysics makes it appropriate now to turn to a new discussion of the relationship between art and toys in the 1980s and 1990s, in which an ironic search for the 'soul of the toy' takes place.

NOTES

29. The classic essay on the art of the 1980s in terms of the dominance of a 'surface' as opposed to 'depth' model of the artist, and in terms of art as fundamentally simulacral, is Fredric Jameson, 'The Cultural Logic of Late Capitalism', in his *Postmodernism, or, The Cultural Logic of Late Capitalism*, Duke University Press, Durham, 1991 (originally published as an article in 1984).
30. Joan Simon, 'Robert Gober and the Extra Ordinary' in *Robert Gober* (exh. cat.), Museo Nacional Centro de Arte Reina Sofia, Madrid, 1991, pp. 18–19.
31. See, for instance, Paul Schimmel, 'Gober is in the Details', in *Robert Gober* (exh. cat.), Museum of Contemporary Arts, Los Angeles, 1997, p. 44.
32. Robert Gober quoted in Theodora Vischer (ed.), *Robert Gober: Sculptures and Installations 1979–2007* (exh. cat.), Schaulager, Basel and Steidl, Göttingen 2007, p. 40.
33. Robert Gober quoted by Elisabeth Sussman in, Theodora Vischer (ed.), op. cit., p. 21.
34. Dave Hickey, 'In the Dancehall of the Dead', in Karen Marta (ed.), *Robert Gober* (exh. cat.), Dia Center for the Arts, New York, 1993.
35. Sussman, op. cit., p. 20.
36. Barthes, op. cit., p. 54.
37. Stuart Morgan, Jutta Koether, David Salle and Sherrie Levine, in 'Big Fun: Four Reactions to the New Jeff Koons', *Artscribe International*, no. 74, March/April, 1989, p. 48.
38. Kirk Varnedoe and Adam Gopnik, *High and Low: Modern Art and Popular Culture* (exh. cat.), The Museum of Modern Art, New York, 1990, p. 396.
39. Stuart Morgan in, 'Big Fun', op. cit., p. 47.
40. Jeff Koons, in an interview with Anthony Hayden-Guest in Angelika Muthesius (ed.), *Jeff Koons*, Taschen, Cologne, 1992, p. 26.
41. Bernd Brunner, *Bears: A Brief History* (trans. Lori Lantz), Yale University Press, New Haven and London, 2007, p. 218.
42. For the teddy bear revival see Michèle Brown, *The Little History of the Teddy Bear*, Sutton Publishing, Stroud, 2001, pp. 150–55.
43. Susan Stewart, *On Longing: Narratives of the Miniature, the Gigantic, the Souvenir, the Collection*, Duke University Press, Durham and London, 1993, pp. 73–4.
44. Brown, op. cit., p. 75.
45. Koons interview, op. cit., p. 26.
46. Koons interview, op. cit., p. 28.

CHAPTER 3

'THE SOUL OF THE TOY'

MIKE KELLEY AND PAUL McCARTHY

The works of Helen Chadwick, Robert Gober and Jeff Koons discussed here reflect an approach to childhood and toys that is bound up with nostalgia or with an attitude of taking stock. It might be argued that this retrospective tendency was symptomatic of the waning twentieth century. The historicity embedded in these artists' works – the harking back to the 1950s or 1960s – could be seen as a retreat from the sheer complexity of adult experience in the 1980s, an explanation that seems simplistic, despite the fact that the 1980s were a challenging decade. For many it was dominated by the AIDS crisis and the return of right-wing governments, whose social policies saw the wealthy become increasingly well-off (with a booming art market in America in particular, especially in the early part of the period) while the lives of the less well-off and the socially marginalised were made increasingly difficult (resulting in race-related riots in England in the early 1980s).

The art historian Hal Foster has characterised one strand of late-1980s art as bound up with a notion of 'abjection', which was often metaphorically expressed as physical revulsion – evident in the widespread imagery of bodily decay and dissolution – at the damage done to the social contract by hard-line conservative administrations. He has applied this concept to Gober's work as well as to that of Mike Kelley and Paul McCarthy. For Foster, the iconography of childhood in their work merely sets up for the artists 'an infantilist persona to mock the paternal order'; they 'probe the wound of trauma', he says, but express 'little more than a fatigue with the politics of difference'.[47] This reading of their work as symptomatic, however, ends up downplaying the critical agency of the artists. The concentration on toys and playthings in *'Childish Things'* hopes to suggest that, through one of the central symbols of the era, artists approached childhood as a terrain on which important issues about the socialisation of children, the discussion of which came to a head in the late-twentieth century, could be dealt with. Indeed the whole relationship between the child and the adult, or the theme of adult-as-child, which takes in the 'extended adolescence' brought about by post-war patterns of parenting, became an issue in a way it had not previously.[48] Kelley and McCarthy's use of the imagery of innards and anatomy might easily be swept under Foster's critical blanket of 'abjection'. In fact, as I will show, Kelley and McCarthy dwell precisely on the child's probing of the inner life of the toy in order to pinpoint a crisis in the attitude of adults to childhood.

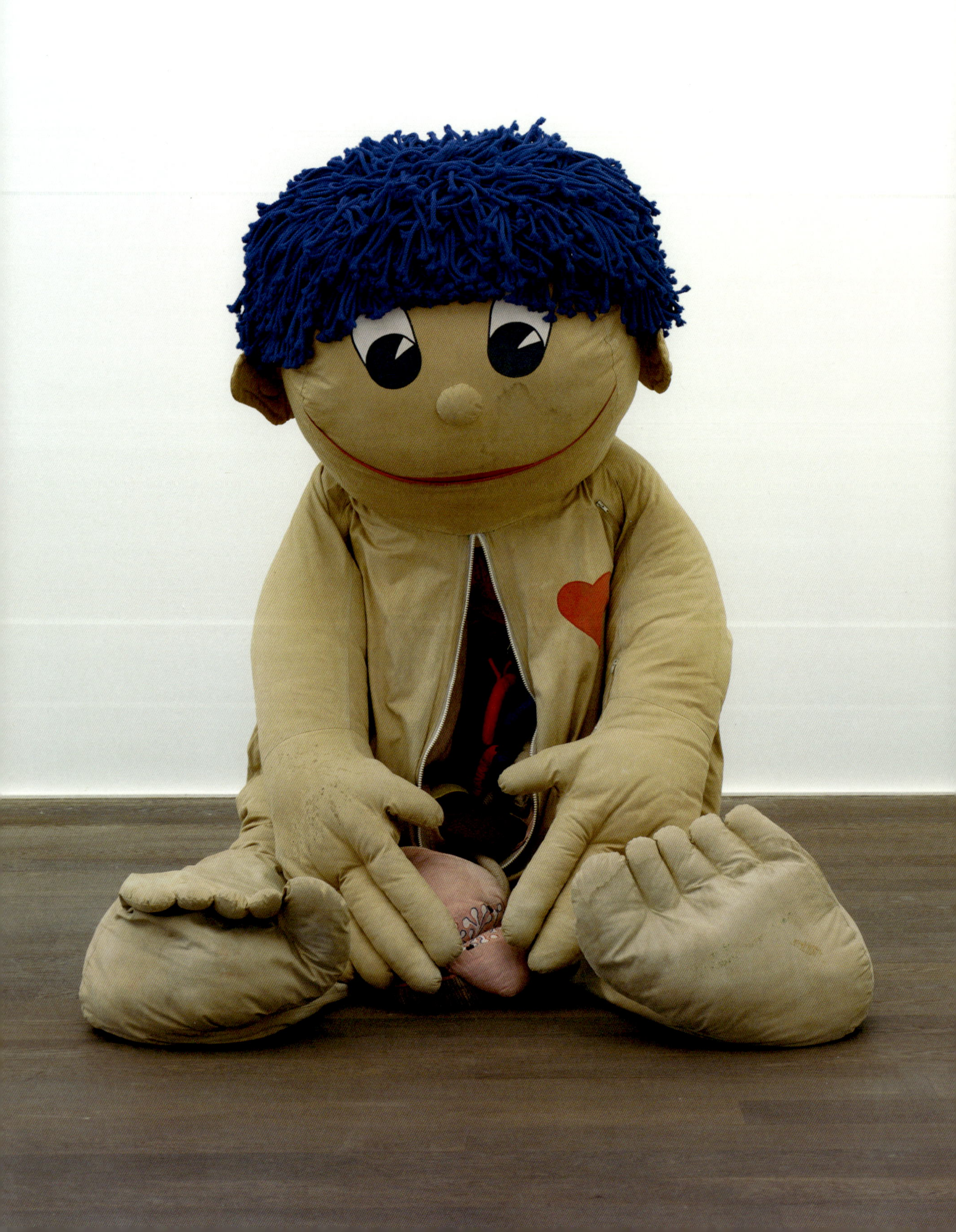

PAUL McCARTHY, *Children's Anatomical Educational Figure*, c. 1990

INNARDS/ANATOMY

In 2004 US artist Mike Kelley curated an exhibition titled 'The Uncanny', at Tate Liverpool and Museum Moderner Kunst Stiftung Ludwig Wien, in which he borrowed a seemingly innocuous object from his friend, and oft-times collaborator in the Los Angeles art scene, Paul McCarthy. The object was a large, dumpy, dopey-looking toy figure, generically related through its woollen hair to the rag-doll puppets of post-1960s British and US television (Andy Pandy would be their grandfather). It might have been innocent enough but for the large zippered gash that spread the length of its body and out of which its soft-toy innards spilled. Significantly, perhaps, it was not a work by the artist, but a readymade, something from a shop which McCarthy had been given by a friend and which his children apparently played with.[49] Titled by McCarthy *Children's Anatomical Educational Figure*, it presumably originated as an educational toy. But it appealed of course to a primordial desire that children have to pull apart their playthings, to reach their depths, to get at their inner workings.

In one of the most insightful essays ever written on the subject of toys the nineteenth-century French poet and critic Charles Baudelaire dwelt on precisely this childish impulse. His ruminations are worth quoting at length:

> The overriding desire of most children is to get at and *see the soul* of their toys … It is on the more or less swift invasion of this desire that depends the length of life of a toy. I do not find it in myself to blame this infantile mania; it is a first metaphysical tendency. When this desire has implanted itself in the child's cerebral marrow, it fills his fingers and nails with an extraordinary agility and strength. The child twists and turns his toy, scratches it, shakes it, bumps it against the walls, throws it on the ground. From time to time, he makes it restart its mechanical motions, sometimes in the opposite direction. Its marvellous life comes to a stop. The child … makes a supreme effort; at last he opens it up, he is the stronger. But *where is the soul*? This is the beginning of melancholy and gloom.[50]

For Baudelaire, then, the toy is something whose essence must be revealed, whose secret life must somehow be laid bare. Play becomes a way to move beyond pleasure into the territory of destruction; a kind of god-like vengeance is visited on the child's hapless plaything. The culmination of this process – the revelation that there is no essence to be plumbed within the recalcitrant object after it has been prised open – leads to the child's first brush with spiritual torpor or emptiness.

It seems to me that the kind of psychological atmosphere suggested so powerfully by Baudelaire has a peculiar resonance with the battered and abused playthings of Kelley and McCarthy. The artists' close affinities, which led them to collaborate on projects such as the harrowing *Family Tyranny* video of 1987, are especially marked in works they produced involving toys. McCarthy had been using toys which were connotative of Disney or other aspects of mass cultural conditioning in his performances from between 1972 and 1984, and these objects (which were stored in trunks and later exhibited in their own right, and photographed for the series *Propo*) bore witness, in their soiled and dilapidated condition, to McCarthy's ceremonial manhandling and desecration of them. By 1987 Kelley was also making assemblages from soiled toys or from conglomerations of hand-knitted dolls which, like McCarthy's work, were often concerned with interpersonal family relations. (At the same time, they challenged sculptural conventions in very incisive ways. For a male artist to predicate his practice on craft-produced or knitted items at this time meant that a dialogue with the feminist revalorisation of crafts and decorative arts techniques was being set up at some level. In this respect Kelley's work in this exhibition sits interestingly alongside Louise Bourgeois's fabric figurines). His floor-based *Arena* pieces, such as *Arena #7 (Bears)* (1990; p. 61) first exhibited in 1990, were especially concerned with contemporary attitudes to infant play and psychology.

PAUL McCARTHY, *Untitled* from *Propo* series (*Donald Duck*), 1972–94

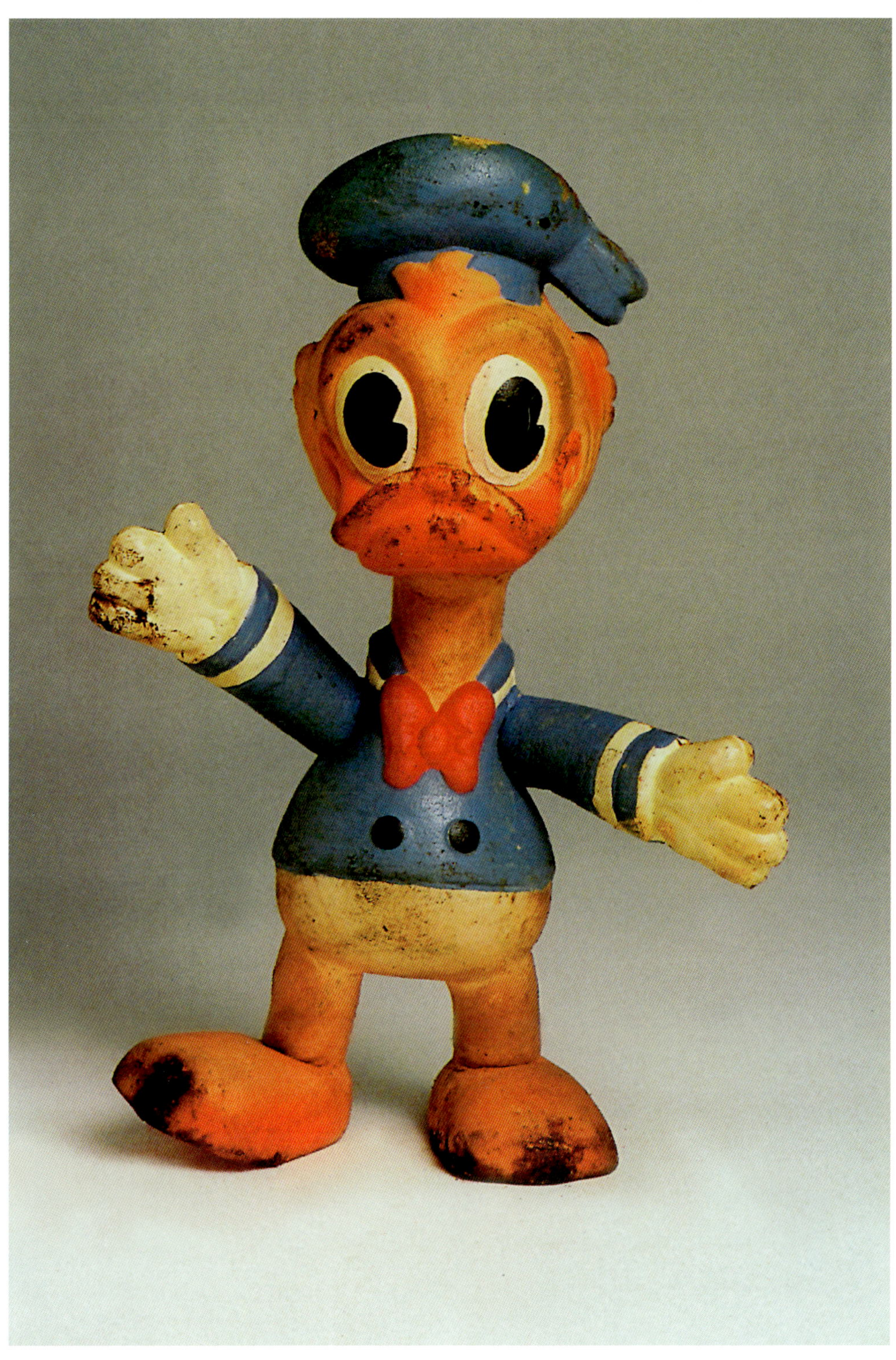

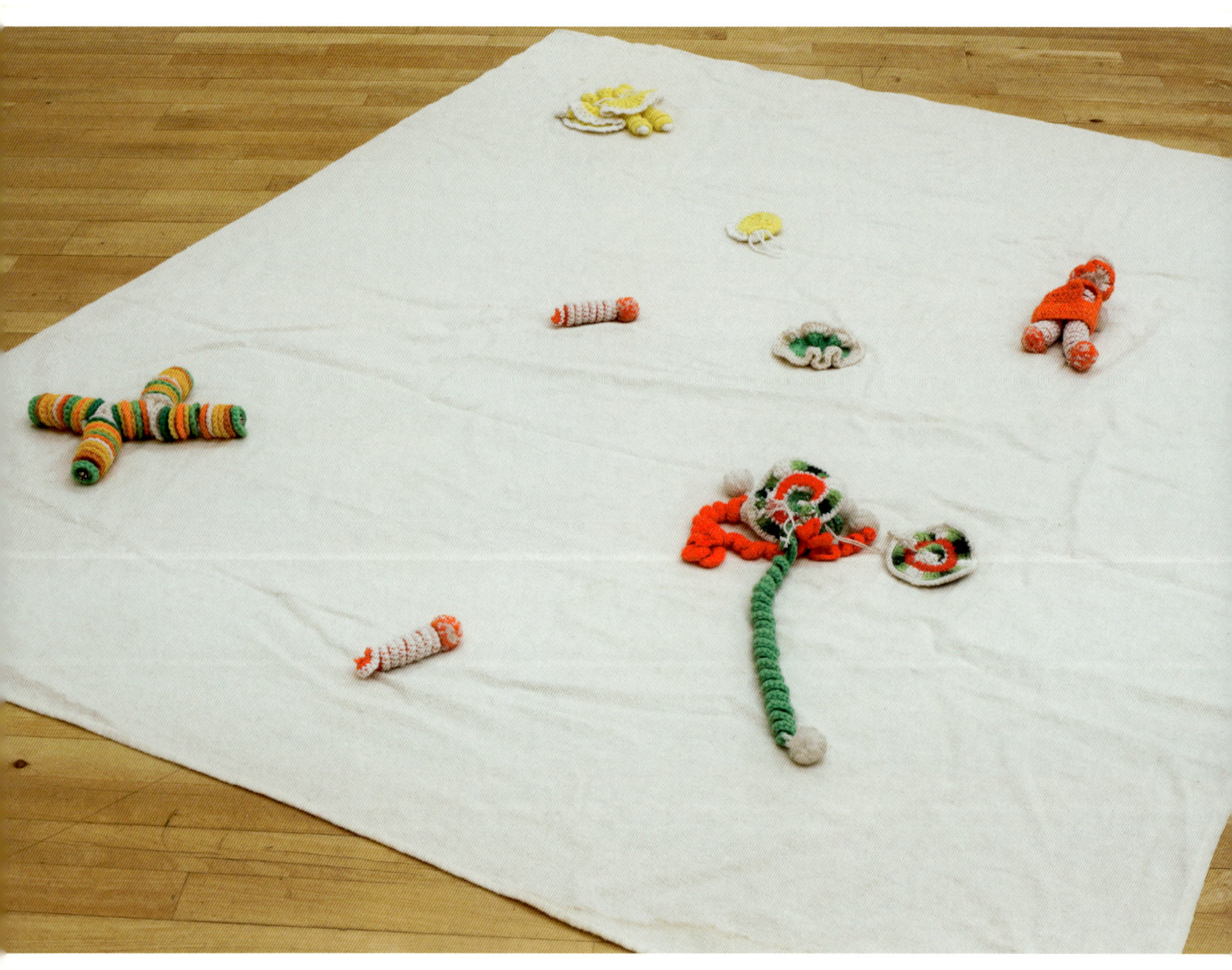

MIKE KELLEY, *Innards*, 1990

Kelley's *Innards*, a work closely related to his *Arena* pieces, comprises a group of knitted woollen objects scattered forlornly on a blanket. On close inspection, they become identifiable as a doll's eviscerated corpse with arms wrenched off, a vestigial anatomy, and a weird composite of phallic forms. Its scenario of dismemberment foregrounds the aggressivity and ferocity of young children, and hints at the Baudelairean melancholy that lies in the aftermath of such destructive orgies (and, closer to Kelley's intentions, their psychoanalytic implications). McCarthy's *Children's Anatomical Educational Figure* also refers to the child's direct penetration into the toy, encouraging some degree of reflection on the investigative drive of infants.

In the early-twentieth century, another classic account of child psychology appeared which, like Baudelaire's narrative of the dawn of metaphysical anxiety, constituted a quest for origins. This was Freud's account of the stirrings of the epistemological impulse in his analysis of Leonardo da Vinci. Trying to make sense of the repression of sexuality and the overestimation of the quest for knowledge in the adult life of Leonardo da Vinci, Freud discerns the roots of this psychological predisposition in children's sexual investigations. Freud states: 'They investigate along their own lines, divine the baby's presence inside the mother's body, and following the lead of the impulses of their own sexuality, form theories of babies originating from eating, of their being born through the bowels, and of the obscure part played by the father.'[51] Freud eventually reasons that the inconclusive nature of such investigations (he writes of 'the failure in the first attempt at intellectual independence') stands at the root of a sense of malaise such that: 'This brooding and doubting becomes the prototype of all later intellectual work directed towards the solution of problems, and the first failure has a crippling effect on the child's whole future.'[52]

Freud then, like Baudelaire, locates a particular quality of frustration, akin to depression, at this early investigative moment. But he goes further in extrapolating mankind's perennial urge-to-knowledge from this early stalling of ambition. Without wishing to suggest that either Freud, or Baudelaire for that matter, are direct points of reference for Kelley or McCarthy, their work circulates around a similar range of issues – namely an interconnectedness between the morbidly destructive impulses of children and their investigative energy. McCarthy's *Children's Anatomical Educational Figure* ruefully indicates that such processes are legitimated socially via the acceptable genre of the 'educational' toy. These toys have been marketed, in a vast variety of forms, in the US and elsewhere since the early-twentieth century, and were especially in vogue in the 1960s and 1970s. The historian Gary Cross notes that the lofty educational principles underlying the objects frequently masked their nature as commodities: 'Advertising reminded parents of the diverse educational needs of children while pushing them to fill the toy box to the brim.'[53] McCarthy implies that such educational aids sometimes trade, in fact, on atavistic instincts. Beyond this, Kelley's works in their wider context set up connections between the emotionally-intense imagery of early childhood and contemporary discourses of education, therapy and child development.

In particular, Kelley's *Arena* series (and related works such as *Innards*) draw on what John Welchman has described as 'object relations and interpersonal dynamics.'[54] We might, for instance, read these floor-based works as oblique references to play situations presided over by a post-Kleinian or Winnicottian psychotherapist of the late-1980s, with the soft toys still humorously appearing to act out roles from a child's symbolic phantasy play. The works, then, are as much about the adult management and conceptualisation of the evolution of the child's mental life as they are about the child's own psychological fantasies, a point underlined by Kelley when he stated:

> One thing I've found about this work is that people are unwilling to think about it in terms of the politics of the adult – no matter how many clues you give them, they always see the work in relation to the child, as if these dolls had something to do with children's desires. But they don't. All this stuff is produced by adults for children, expressing adult ideas about the reality of children.[55]

Kelley's talk of 'adult ideas about the reality of children' helps to make the kind of artistic engagement with playthings that I am exploring more historically specific. In Britain and the US the 1980s and 1990s were a period when, in the wake of the liberalism of the 1960s and 1970s,

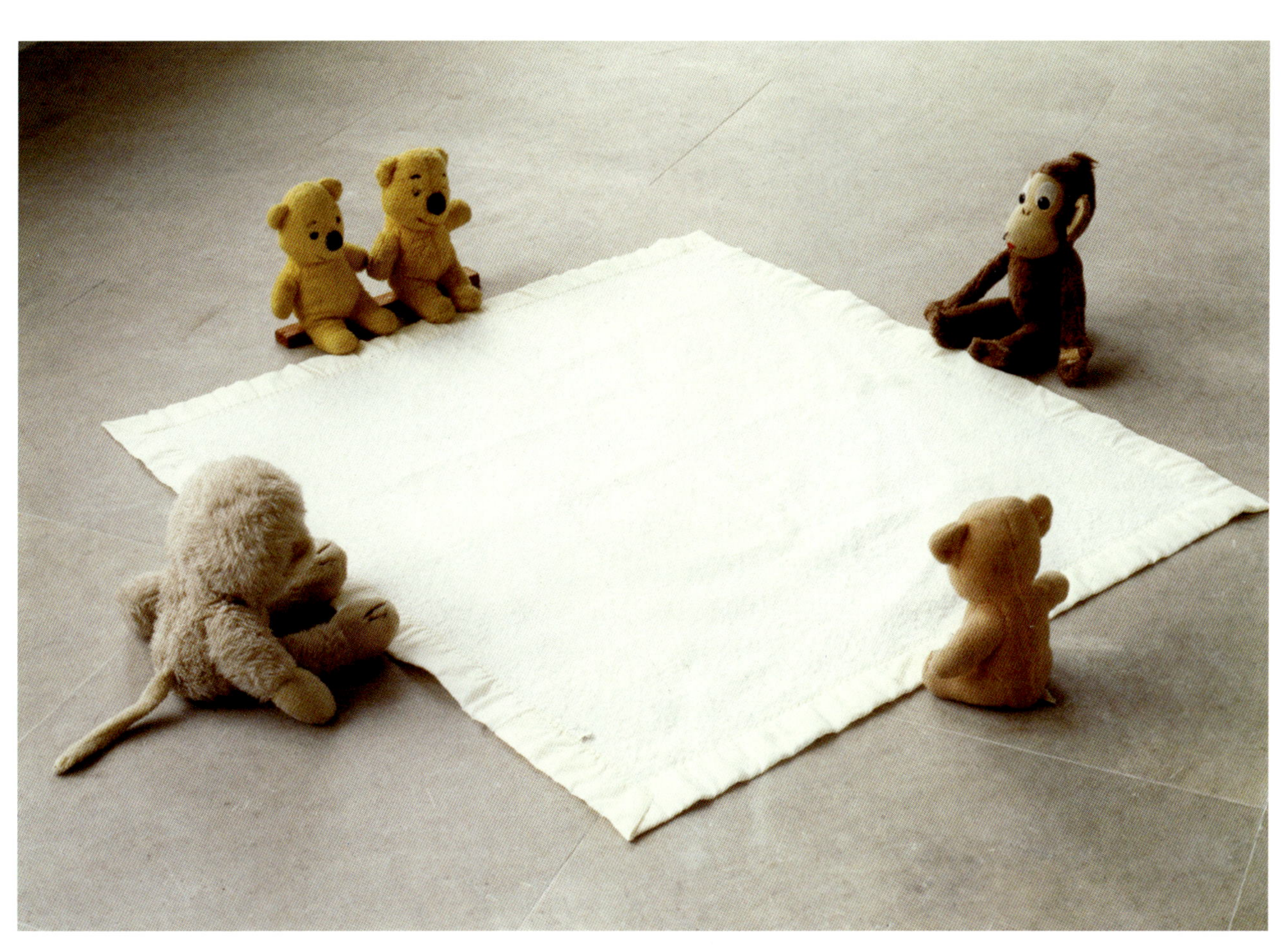

MIKE KELLEY, *Arena #7 (Bears)*, 1990

a new moralism and legalism came into being regarding children and childhood, in line with the right-wing agenda of the time. An enormous amount of public attention was channelled into the issue of children's vulnerability, and more specifically to the prevalence of child abuse, with debates relating to children's social welfare and psychological well-being leading to major revisions of the legal system. In Britain the 'Children Act' of 1989 can be seen as encapsulating a conservative reaction to the moral panics that punctuated the 1980s, notably the Cleveland child abuse scandal of 1987 in which 121 cases of suspected child sexual abuse were diagnosed by two paediatricians at a Middlesbrough hospital, of which 96 were dismissed by the courts. Turning to the American context, Kelley himself has been heavily engaged with the issue of repressed memory syndrome, which stimulated a fierce debate in the US in the late 1980s and early 1990s. He elaborates on this at some length, in relation to his ongoing *Missing Time* project, in a catalogue text of 1995:

> The project grew out of my interest in a debate raging in the United States over the issue of repressed memory syndrome, which, simply stated, is the notion that memories of traumatic experiences can be completely and unconsciously blocked out and made inaccessible to the conscious mind. In recent years a large therapeutic industry has emerged working on the assumption that childhood sexual abuse is the cause of this syndrome. Such therapists also believe that repressed memories can be recalled through therapy and that remembering them can help cure patients of a variety of symptoms, the most serious of which is multiple personality disorder. Many therapists who champion the idea of repressed memory syndrome believe that all memories dredged up during therapy are true. This is the kernel of the debate: one camp defends the notion that in almost all cases recalled memories of childhood sexual abuse are historically true, while another camp argues that these memories are often fantasies, or are even unwittingly implanted in the patient by the therapists themselves.[56]

This concept of repressed memory syndrome, which revisits Freud's notorious difficulties with his early seduction theory and its abandonment in 1897 in favour of a model of fantasised parental seduction, was given its most polemical expression in a book by Ellen Bass and Laura David of 1988 titled *The Courage to Heal* and then by Renee Fredrickson in *Repressed Memories: A Journey to Recovery from Sexual Abuse* in 1992. It was largely discredited by a spate of publications of the mid-1990s, but had already helped secure the conviction of several alleged abusers in the US in the early 1990s on the basis of the victims' memory recovery, rather than demonstrable physical evidence.

Kelley's own response to this climate of suspicion has been far-reaching. Given that a number of critics of the early 1990s had mistakenly interpreted his soft toys works as dealing with what they imagined to be his own background of abuse, Kelley came to thematize his art activity specifically in therapeutic terms. Hence he says:

> I always assumed that my current work must in some way be affected by my art training, even though I rebelled against this education and saw no particular formal relation between recent and student work. The 'symptoms' of my recent work must, then, be the by-product of elements of my training that I have repressed. Further, this repression proves my training must have been traumatic – it must have been a form of abuse.[57]

The ingeniously twisted logic of this assertion lies at the root of several significant works by Kelley. In 1995 he exhibited a group of *Works on Paper 1974–1976* – works produced in other words during the years of initial artistic training – which he had painted over or reworked in the 1990s, as though conducting a form of auto-analysis. In the same year he produced a mock-architectural model titled *Educational Complex* which more comprehensively elaborated a fictionalised account of the so-called abuse underlying his art. The model dealt with Kelley's failure to recall aspects of his own formative educational development. Describing it, he asserted that it was 'made up of every school I have ever attended, with the sections I cannot remember left blank. The blank sections are supposedly the result of some "trauma" that occurred in those spots, which has caused me to repress them.'[58]

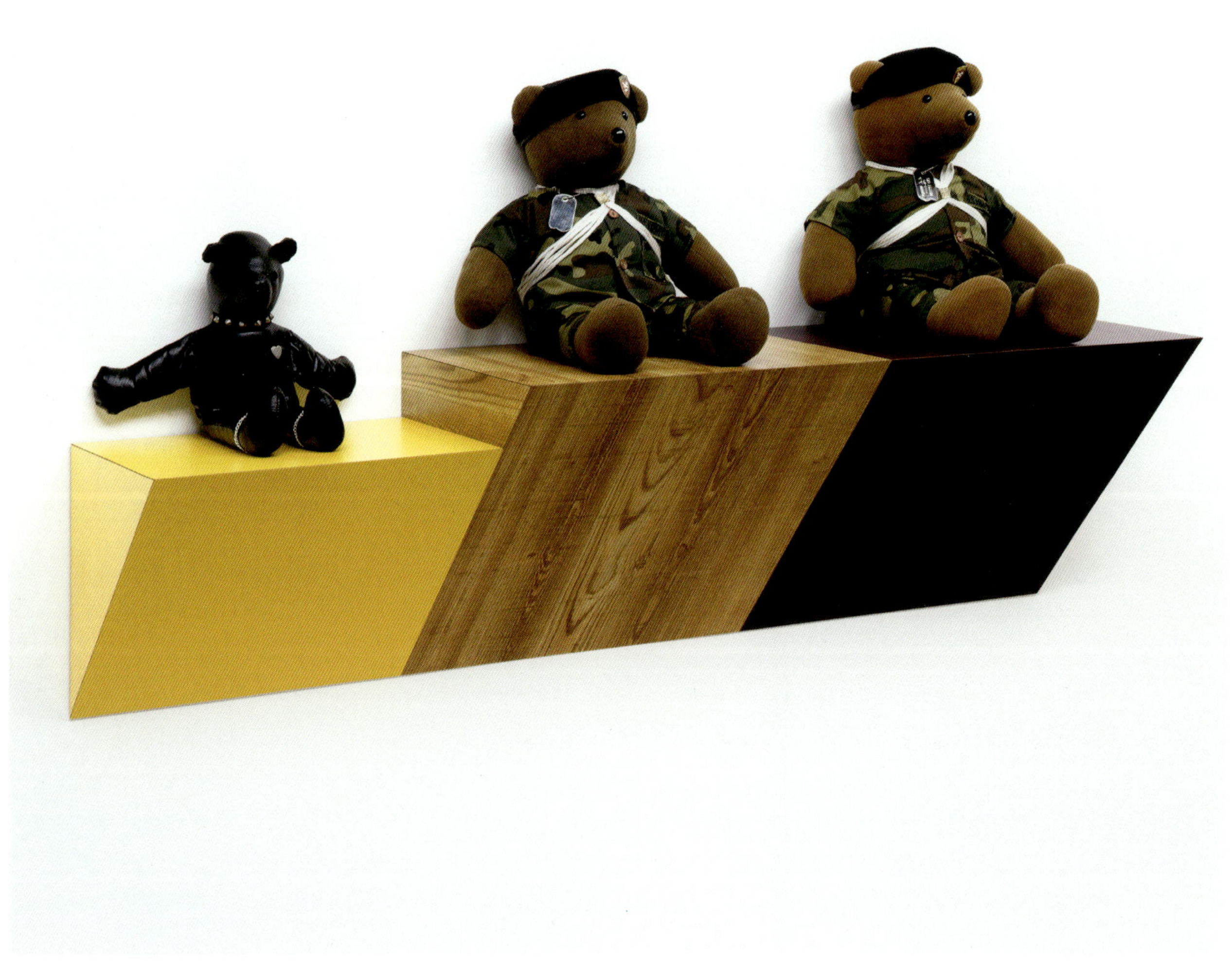

Quite apart from the mock-psychologistic thematisation of Kelley's artistic training here, one is reminded of the Freudian correlation between the repression of childish sexual curiosity and the compensatory value placed on investigation or research, which Kelley could easily be parodying.

It is clear that both Kelley and McCarthy's work of the early 1990s responds to an atmosphere of anxiety regarding processes of children's upbringing, socialisation, psychological development and so forth. One of the ironies of my recourse to Freud up until now is that the two artists came to maturity in an epoch in which classical Freudianism had been completely overhauled by the so-called post-Freudians – by Klein, Winnicott and their followers – a period in which the practice of child psychotherapy had become thoroughly institutionalised, and in which the more esoteric theorisations of Klein *et al.* were being generalized and annexed to cruder social and political agendas; hence the hysteria over repressed memory syndrome. Kelley and McCarthy's sculptures are extremely ironic in relation to the socialisation of children in the 1990s but also highly attentive to the way psychotherapeutic discourses themselves inflect and invade the imagery they are meant to comment on. In this context Kelley's *Innards*, with its allusions to a therapeutic session in which a child is invited to act out its darker fantasies, might be seen as playing knowingly with Kleinian ideas about the fantasised destruction of the mother's insides.[59] Kelley's work is thus parodic, although ambivalently so, of late-twentieth century American obsessions with child abuse and 'correct' psychological development. His blankets and knitted toys are clearly as much bound up with critiquing contemporary discourses of childhood as they are with childish fantasy itself. In his best work it is hard to separate out Kelley's investment in his subject matter from his critique of its societal institutionalisation.

HAIM STEINBACH, *basics*, 1986

The social and historical context in which Kelley and McCarthy's work has been placed might, of course, be extended to the other artists we have been considering, particularly Helen Chadwick and Robert Gober. This in turn suggests that we should recap here on the art historical framework in which Kelley's and McCarthy's work was produced. In contrast to the toy imagery of the early twentieth-century – from the Surrealists to the Pop artists – which often kept in place the reverie and wonder of the child – the toy/child here is presented as *adulterated* (to introduce an apt pun) by adult discourse. At the same time, it is important to see Kelley and McCarthy as responding to the notion of the toy-as-commodity which was a defining motif in the most publicly visible art, especially on the American East Coast, in the period in which they came to prominence. There can be little doubt that one of the principal reference points for both of them was the toy imagery of Haim Steinbach and Jeff Koons, as already discussed. In an age when spending on toys rose dramatically (from $6.7 billion in 1980 to some $17 billion in 1994[60]), artists such as Steinbach and Koons were extremely important in developing a modern iconography of the toy in which the desires and drives of the child were implicitly correlated with the flows and currents of capitalism. But at the same time, as appropriationists linked to the 1980s art boom, these were paradigmatically 'blue chip' artists, and Kelley and McCarthy's art was developed in strategic counterpoint to theirs. Welchman notes that Kelley's worn and soiled toys engage in a specific dialogue with the enshelved readymade commodity objects of Steinbach: 'Moving from Steinbach to Kelley', writes Welchman, 'allows us to trace the difference between the abstraction and concretion of exchange, predicated on symmetrical moves from hands-on to hands-off production'. Hence: 'Steinbach's objects radiate iconic prestige, and upward mobility; Kelley's are worn, discarded and inept.'[61]

The nostalgic dimension of Koons's work is made even more pronounced alongside the work of Kelley and McCarthy. Both artists work in direct opposition to Koons's practice, countering the relative 'innocence' of his vision – with its associated hankering after metaphysical comforts – with their soiled and abject playthings, adulterated with psychological theory and with the imposition of social anxieties. Theirs are melancholy practices, in the way in which we considered the topos of the child's stunted ambition earlier in relation to Baudelaire and Freud. The toy for them is not so much symbolic of the child's apprehension of freedom as a signifier of the way adults socialise children. Or else, perhaps, it is a weird merger of the two.

NOTES

47. Hal Foster, *The Return of the Real: The Avant-Garde at the End of the Century*, The MIT Press, Cambridge, Massachusetts and London, 1996, pp. 157, 159, 164. His entire discussion is important, see pp. 153–168.
48. David Hopkins, *Dada's Boys: Masculinity After Duchamp*, Yale University Press, New Haven and London, 2007, p. 192 and passim.
49. Information supplied by Paul McCarthy. My thanks to Karin Seinsoth for acting as intermediary.
50. Charles Baudelaire, 'A Philosophy of Toys' (1853), reprinted in, *The Painter of Modern Life and Other Essays* (trans. Jonathan Mayne), Da Capo Press, New York, 1964, pp. 202–3.
51. Sigmund Freud, 'Leonardo da Vinci and a Memory of his Childhood' (1910), reprinted in *The Pelican Freud Library*, vol. 14 (trans. Alan Tyson), Penguin, Harmondsworth, 1985, pp. 168–69.
52. Ibid., p. 169, and see note 1.
53. Gary Cross, *Kids' Stuff: Toys and the Changing World of American Childhood*, Harvard University Press, Cambridge, Massachusetts, 1997, p. 145.
54. John C. Welchman, *Art After Appropriation: Essays on Art in the 1990s*, G+B Arts International, London, 2001, p. 44.
55. Ralph Rugoff, 'Dirty Toys: Mike Kelley Interviewed' in Thomas Kellein, *Mike Kelley*, Kunsthalle Basel and Hajte Cantz, Ostfildern 1992, p. 87.
56. Mike Kelley, 'Missing Time: Works on Paper 1974–1976, Reconsidered' in, John C. Welchman (ed.) *Mike Kelley, Minor Histories: Statements, Conversations, Proposals*, The MIT Press, Cambridge Massachusetts and London, 2004, p. 61.
57. Ibid., p. 62.
58. Mike Kelley in conversation with Isabelle Graw, in *Mike Kelley*, Phaidon Press, London, 1999, p. 19.
59. See, for instance, Melanie Klein, 'The Importance of Symbol Formation in the Development of the Ego' (1930) in Juliet Mitchell, *The Selected Melanie Klein*, op. cit., note 7, pp. 95–111.
60. Cross, op. cit., 1997, p. 189.
61. Welchman, *Art After Appropriation*, op. cit., pp. 43–44.

CHAPTER 4

ADULTERATION

SUSAN HILLER
AND PAUL McCARTHY

The overlaying of adult discourse onto the child's viewpoint to produce a hybrid – for which I have employed the punning term 'adulteration' (which, of course, implies the corruption of the one by the addition of the other) – can be seen as a theme in some of the most powerful works of the 1980s and early 1990s. This surely reflects a crisis in the way children are socialised in so far as we no longer believe it is appropriate to sentimentalise the idea of childhood as a state of purity or innocence (as, say, the Victorians did), but are constantly appalled at the way in which adult life intrudes on its domain (hence the social hysteria in the 1990s regarding paedophilia, child abuse and so on). We project onto children our anxieties. They project back at us what we lack.

Our inability as a society to maintain boundaries between the adult and the infantile or childish is reflected in the very structures of some of the works discussed; Helen Chadwick's *Ego Geometria Sum*, for instance, in which the artist's adult self attempts to align itself with its childish predecessor, or Jeff Koons's child's ornaments, in which small or insignificant items are blown up to an adult's scale. This confusion of the positions of adult and child seems particularly evident in the powerful video and film works, by Susan Hiller and Paul McCarthy respectively, which stand in counterpoint to each other in 'Childish Things'. Both seem to address ideas about our collective understanding of childhood at the end of the twentieth century, if indeed we are able to achieve any distance from it.

PUNCH AND JUDY

Born in the US in 1940, Susan Hiller has lived in Britain since the late 1960s. It is therefore interesting to see her work in this exhibition positioned alongside her American and British peers. Her work has its roots in the conceptualism of the 1970s, and is profoundly eclectic in its utilisation of diverse materials and methods, ranging from displays of postcards (in *Dedicated to the Unknown Artist*, 1972–76) to vitrine displays of natural and cultural objects in boxes (in *From the Freud Museum*, 1991–97). In terms of its prioritisation of intellectual concerns over questions of style, Hiller's work is far closer to the younger Helen Chadwick's than to, say, Jeff Koons's, which looks

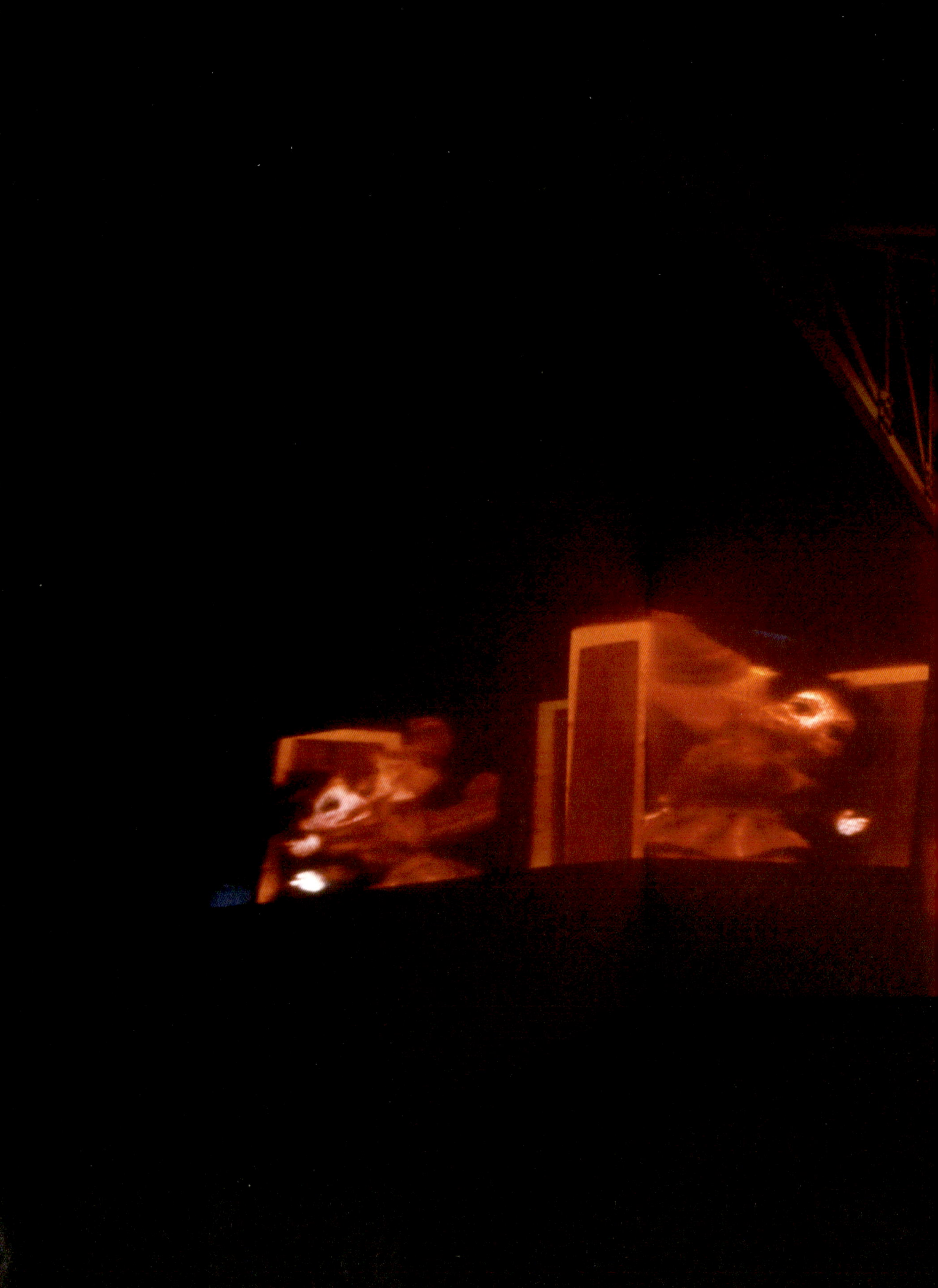

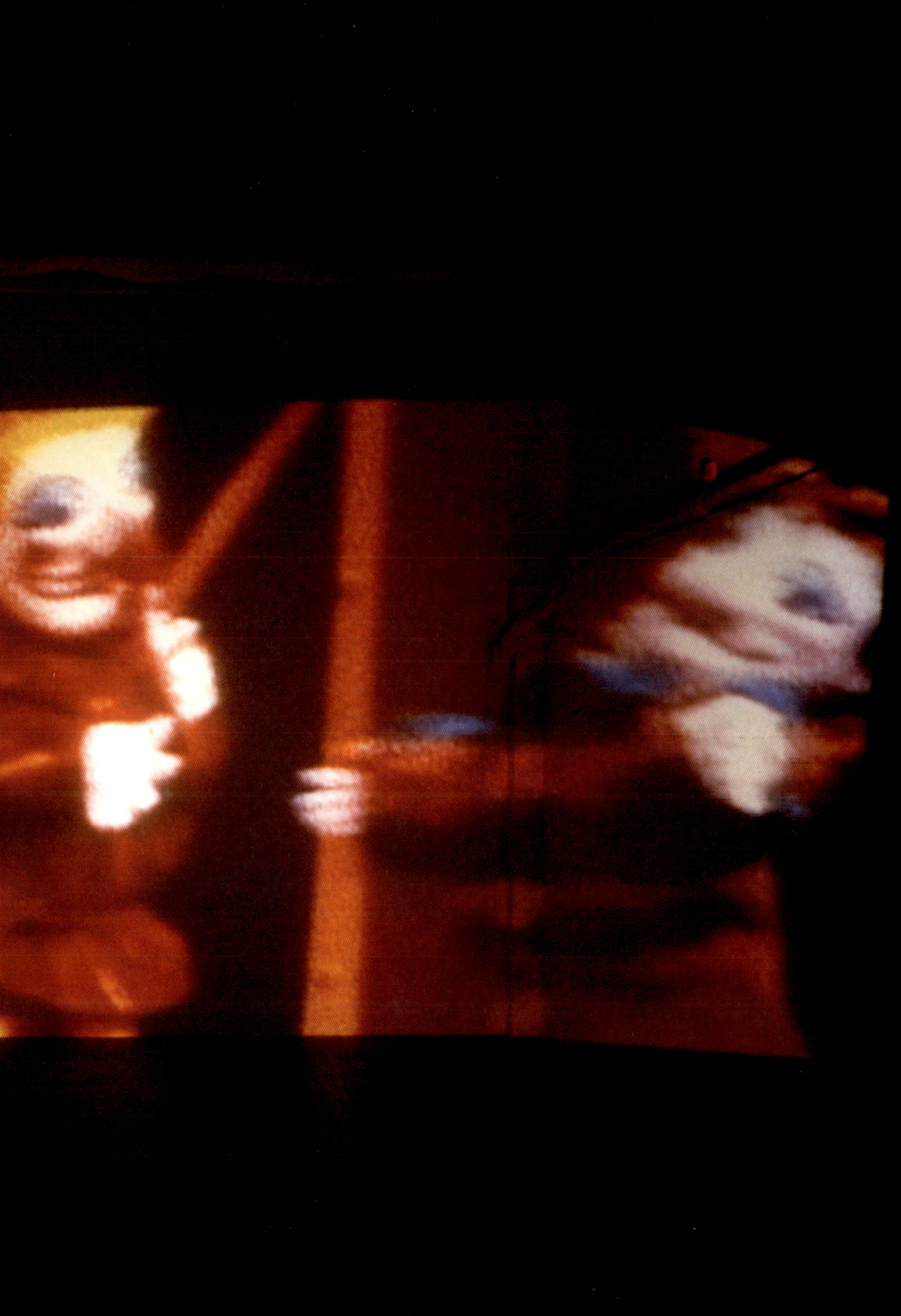

deeply traditional by comparison. Hiller was originally trained as an anthropologist and *An Entertainment* an installation of four synchronised video programmes of 1990, represents a form of anthropological exploration, not so much of toys, but of children's entertainment (although the Punch and Judy puppets that feature in the work are clearly toy-like). Produced around the same time that Mike Kelley was producing his *Arena* series and soiled-toy assemblages, Hiller's work differs markedly from his in aesthetic terms, but shows a similar preoccupation with a dark poetics of childhood. Along with Kelley and McCarthy's works Hiller's *An Entertainment* opens onto the issue of childhood 'ferocity'.

Highly technically innovative when it was first made, *An Entertainment* makes use of four video projectors which project massive, coloured images across the walls of a large, box-like space. These images, which include a skull, a skeleton and a crocodile, as well as images of Punch and his wife, were derived from footage filmed by the artist at Punch and Judy shows in various locations in Britain in the 1980s. Early viewers of the piece – in venues such as Tate Gallery where it was shown in the 1995 'Rites of Passage' exhibition – spoke of their complete disorientation on entering a darkened space and being dwarfed by images which flashed up unexpectedly. Guy Brett brilliantly evokes the general tenor of the experience:

> A flash of red clothing, a noose jerked awkwardly up the wall, a pale flat skull, the relentless violence of the recurrent beatings which become almost like an abstraction of pain: all these images enter the bright arena and disappear in the darkness again.[62]

The adult viewer is placed in the position of a child who must make sense of images of violence while, at the same time, accepting the idea that this ritualised spectacle constitutes entertainment.

previous pages and opposite: SUSAN HILLER, *An Entertainment*, 1990

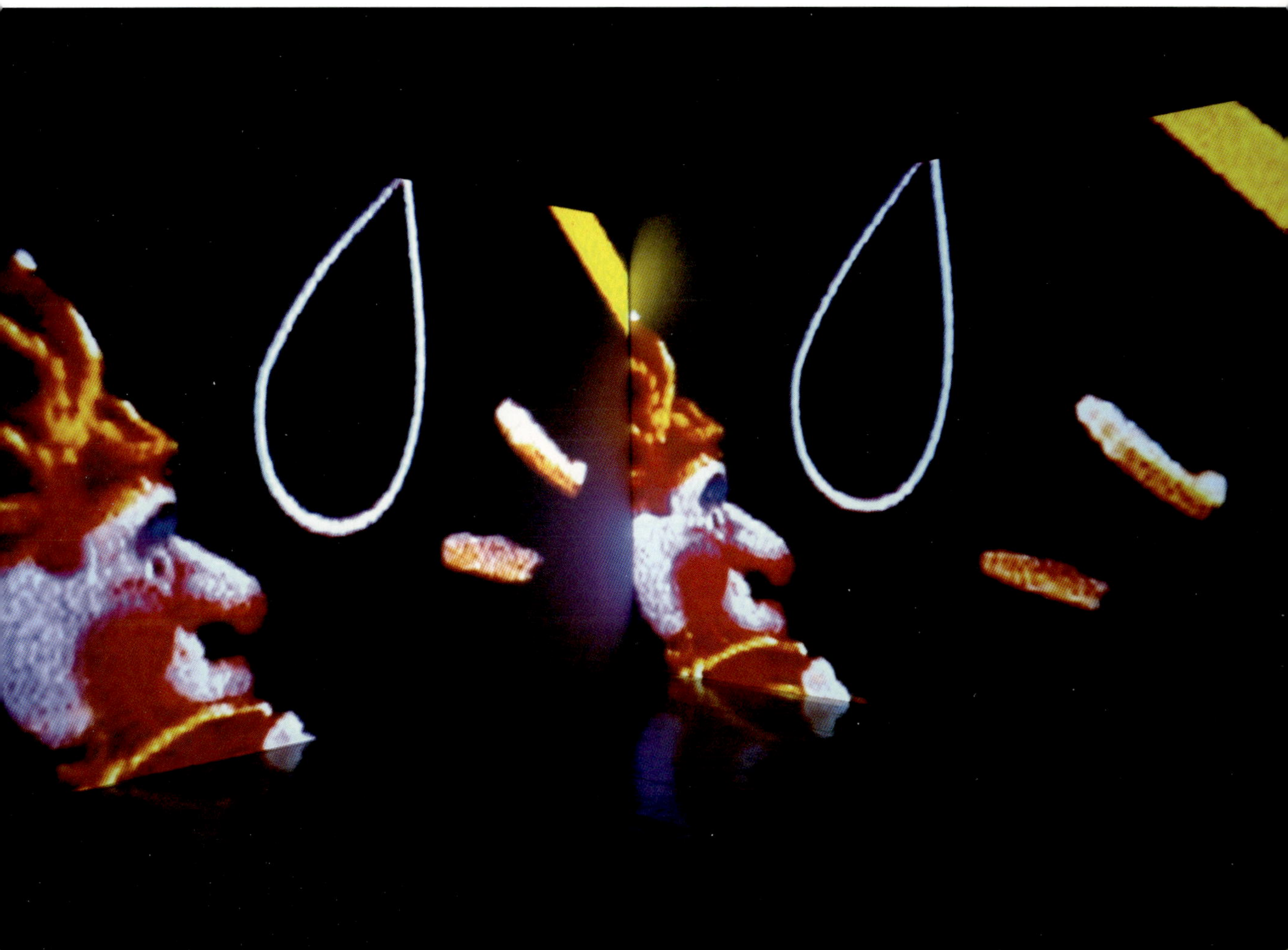

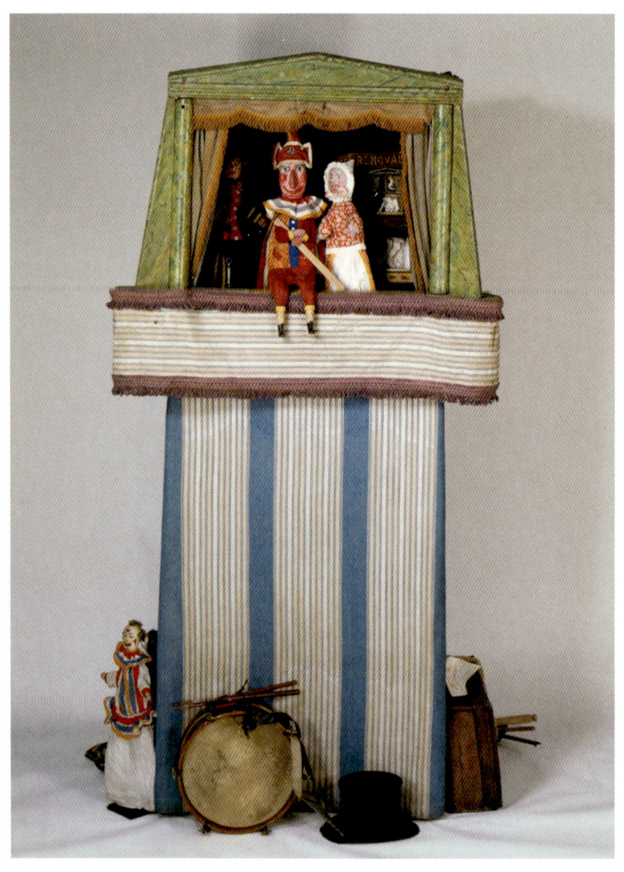

As Hiller explains: 'I was subjecting myself to what I saw children being subjected to with every Punch and Judy show. Yet, at the same time, adults find these little figures hitting each other strangely jolly … the child is being taught something through the terror of ritual.'[63]

It is interesting to speculate as to whether Hiller's work, however different it may be from the contemporaneous work of Kelley, might also be indexed to the social preoccupations with child welfare and psychology discussed earlier in relation to his work. If repressed memory syndrome were being thematised to any degree here, it would be on a racial or cultural level, in so far as the piece probes the traumatic vestiges of what is an ancient social practice, dating back as far as the sixteenth century when Punch was born in Italy as Pulcinella. In Britain, Punch has always been admired as an anarchic 'lord of misrule': Tony Sarg, an American puppeteer of the 1920s and 1930s says:

> Once, in my childhood, I saw the redoubtable hero in his gilded booth … There he strutted, Punch the immortal, untarnished, unchanged. There he crowed his braggart songs, wielded his club, thwacked heads royally, murdered his wife and children and the policeman … and there he hanged the hangman with the noose intended for his own neck, and beat the Devil to death with his cudgel.[64]

Punch and Judy puppet booth, c. 1912

Hiller has talked about wishing to retrieve a collective memory in her work: 'What I am always trying to do, I suppose, is to bring into view those areas which are repressed socially and culturally, those areas which we do in fact share, and to retrieve for all of us ... a sense of ourselves, as part of a collective.'[65] As Mr Punch repeatedly beats his wife and child, his formulaic chants, 'That's the way to do it' and so on, are reiterated by a voice on the soundtrack as though being translated from a forgotten or unfamiliar language, and this in itself subtly metaphoricises the surfacing of repressed unconscious materials. But one should be careful of making the piece sound too one-dimensional. Many other issues are at stake here. Hiller has spoken interestingly about the relationship between left-handedness and right-handedness in terms of the way puppeteers manipulate Punch and Judy puppets. This structural split was instituted when the tradition was transported from Italy to Britain in the eighteenth century and glove puppets rather than marionettes were employed. As Hiller wryly observes, '[this] improved the fights: you can pit your right hand against the left so well.'[66] She goes on to extrapolate a fascinating piece of analysis from this:

> As society becomes increasingly rational we've tended to downgrade the intuitive. Punch and Judy puts Punch on the puppeteer's dominant right hand – and all the other characters, women, children, animals, death – on the intuitive, denigrated left. As in ancient myth it reduces to a dualism, which may refer as much to these opposed parts of our brain and body as to anything socio-historical.[67]

Hiller's *An Entertainment* could be correlated with Koons's *Bear and Policeman* and *Winter Bears* in terms of this concern with the folkloric, which suggests that it also harbours a certain nostalgia; but Hiller is more probing as to the ongoing cultural consequences of her imagery. In this respect, it is perhaps not surprising that she has suggested that parental abuse may be a significant aspect of the work:

> The baby-battering, wife-beating, homicidal violence of the central character too clearly reflects the actual conditions of patriarchy, and the emphatic centrality of the nuclear family and domestic setting emphasise what is commonly known but universally denied.[68]

SUSAN HILLER, *Clair de Lune II*, 1985

Without ruling out the other levels of meanings which are clearly present, her work may in this sense be keyed to the political atmosphere of Britain at this time; to the 1989 Children Act passed by the Thatcher government which paid official lip service to the moral panics of the previous decade, and more particularly to some of the cases themselves. The series of allegations of satanic ritual abuse are particularly pertinent here (the most notorious case being the Orkney Islands scandal of the late 1980s in which nine children were removed from their families until the case was thrown out of court after a single day of evidence. Over-zealous social workers were eventually held to account for sparking the allegations).

Hiller's work may well be seen as an investigation of a collective imaginary in which children were continually held to be at the mercy of supernatural, archaic forces. Given that the very figure of Punch epitomises Englishness (the Victorian magazine *Punch* attests to his national prominence), the entire piece might also be seen as linked, highly ironically, to the chauvinistic mood of late Thatcherism. The work's ferocity lies in the sense in which we are rendered powerless as spectators by the unruly archetypes paraded before us, which are archetypes of regression returning us, via the figure of Punch, to the destructiveness of the drives — to temper tantrums and fantasies of omnipotence. This ferocity has an anarchic edge, and the standpoint of the piece is hard to gauge.

One feels invaded in some way, and in this sense parallels can be made with Hiller's mid-1980s ripolin on wallpaper works such as *Claire de Lune II* (1985) or *Masters of the Universe* (1986) in which the artist overlays her automatic writing onto sheets of children's wallpaper so that what Lucy Lippard describes as 'idiot ideological images' – Lippard calls them 'vacuous Pierrots and cute bombers' – are translated from the walls of the playroom into some indecipherable language of the unconscious, and simultaneously invested with a more frenetic energy as they are metaphorically drawn out from the wall.[69] These works, like *An Entertainment*, seem to question whether it is possible to separate our adult selves from our childish selves, in so far as we are ruled by unconscious imperatives that have little regard for age.

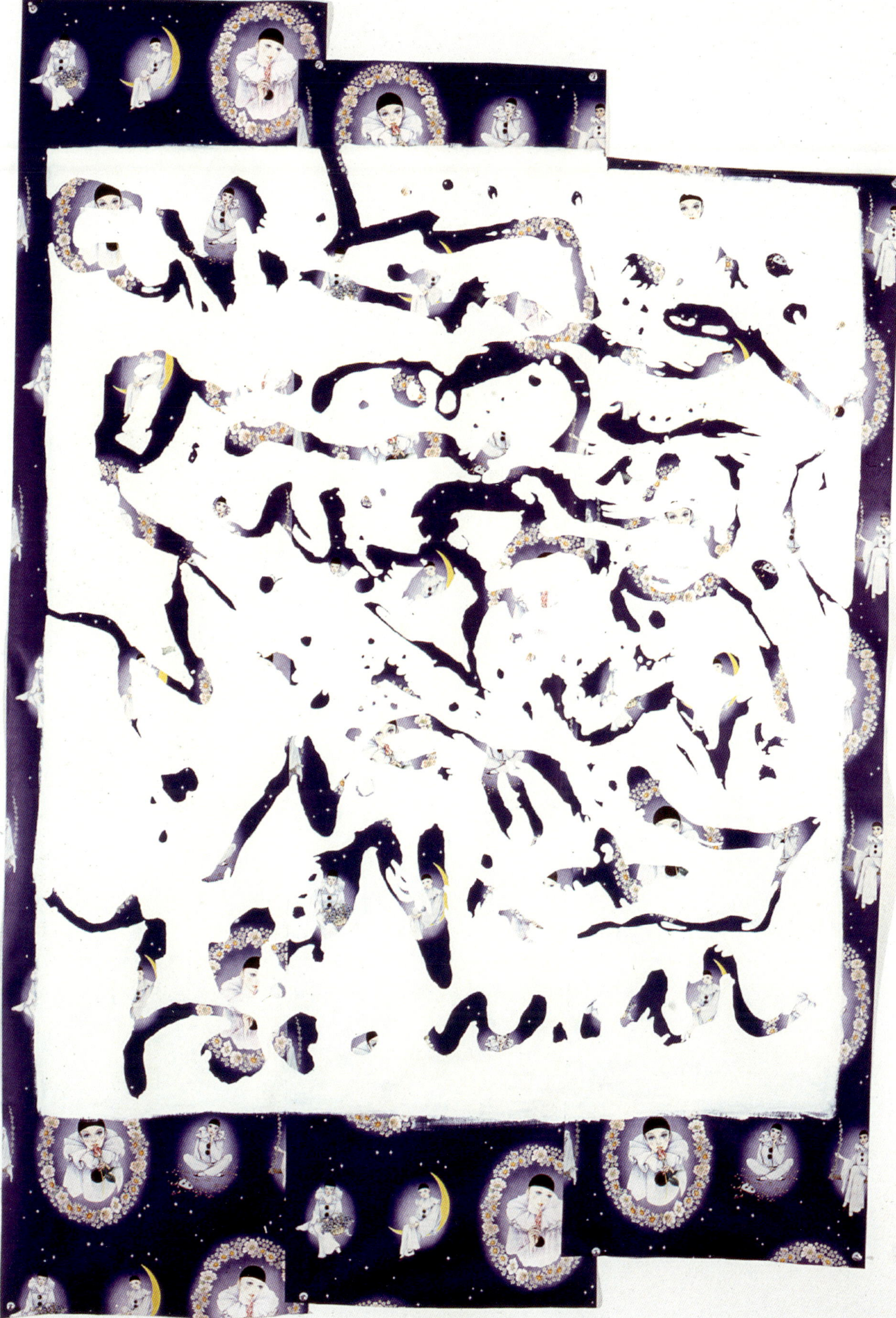

'THE SOUND OF MUSIC'

In 1965, at the age of ten, I sat with my parents in a cinema in Derby and watched *The Sound of Music*. Although it felt special, for such occasions were rare, it was not in any way unique; thousands of families all over Britain and the US were doing the same thing. The film, a musical by Rogers and Hammerstein starring Julie Andrews, which had come out that year, was a great box-office success. The American artist Paul McCarthy, who was then twenty, could not have failed to have been aware of the film nor, perhaps, to have cringed at what for many people of his age would have been its almost unbearable sweetness. One critic at the time, who was allegedly fired for her directness, called it 'a sugar-coated lie that people seem to want to eat.'[70] In 2001, McCarthy re-presented *The Sound of Music* in Austria as *cisuM fo dnuoS ehT*, with the film played backwards and upside-down, although run at normal speed. Along with his *Children's Anatomical Educational Figure*, it constitutes his second 'readymade' contribution to 'Childish Things' (although *The Sound of Music*, unlike the anatomical model, has obviously been tampered with by McCarthy quite considerably).

The Sound of Music represented a panacea for anxieties about the disintegration of the family in middle America in the mid-1960s, and the BBC in Britain even decreed some years later that its soundtrack should be broadcast on radio to reassure the public in the event of a nuclear attack.[71] The plot recounts the story of the arrival of a trainee nun (Maria, played by Andrews) as a governess in the service of a wealthy Austrian, Captain von Trapp (played by Christopher Plummer). Transforming the lives of his seven children by encouraging their singing talents, and winning the heart of their gloomy widower father, she leads the family to happiness and fulfilment despite the intervention of historical events in the form of the Nazi entry into Austria, that threatens their perfect family life.

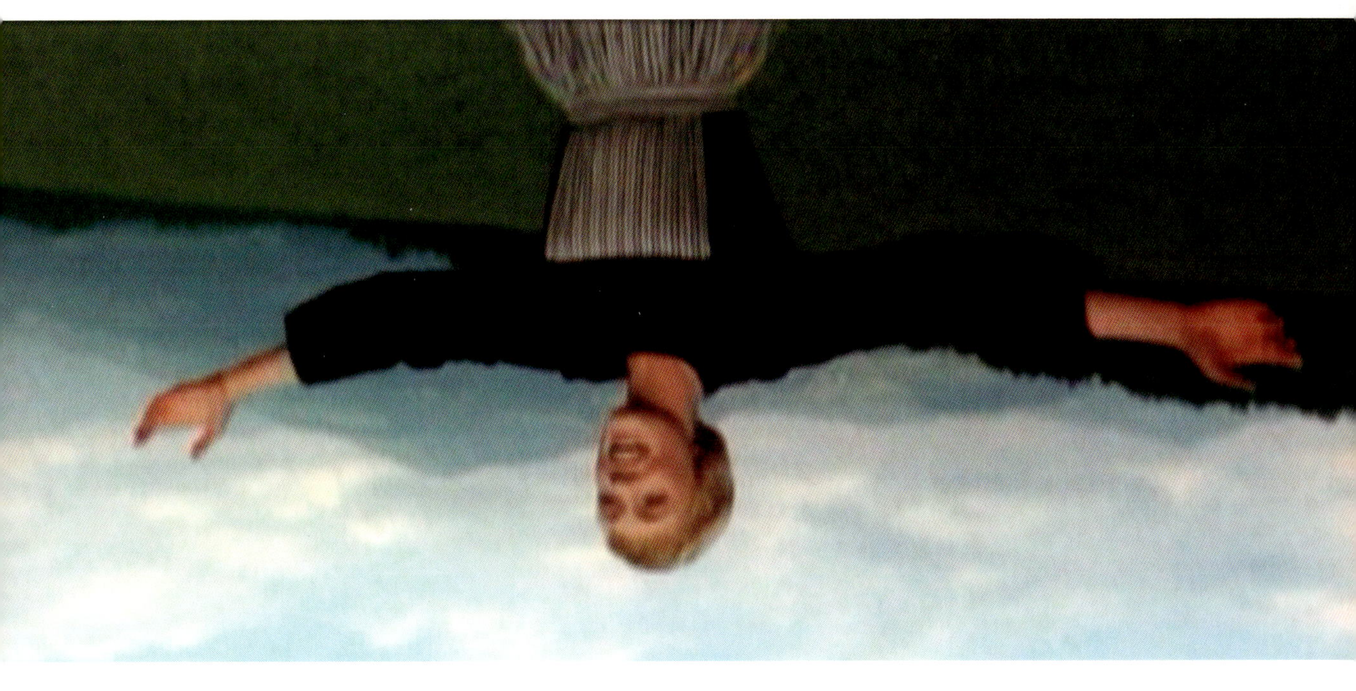

PAUL McCARTHY, *cisuM fo dnuoS ehT / The Sound of Music*, 2008 (still)

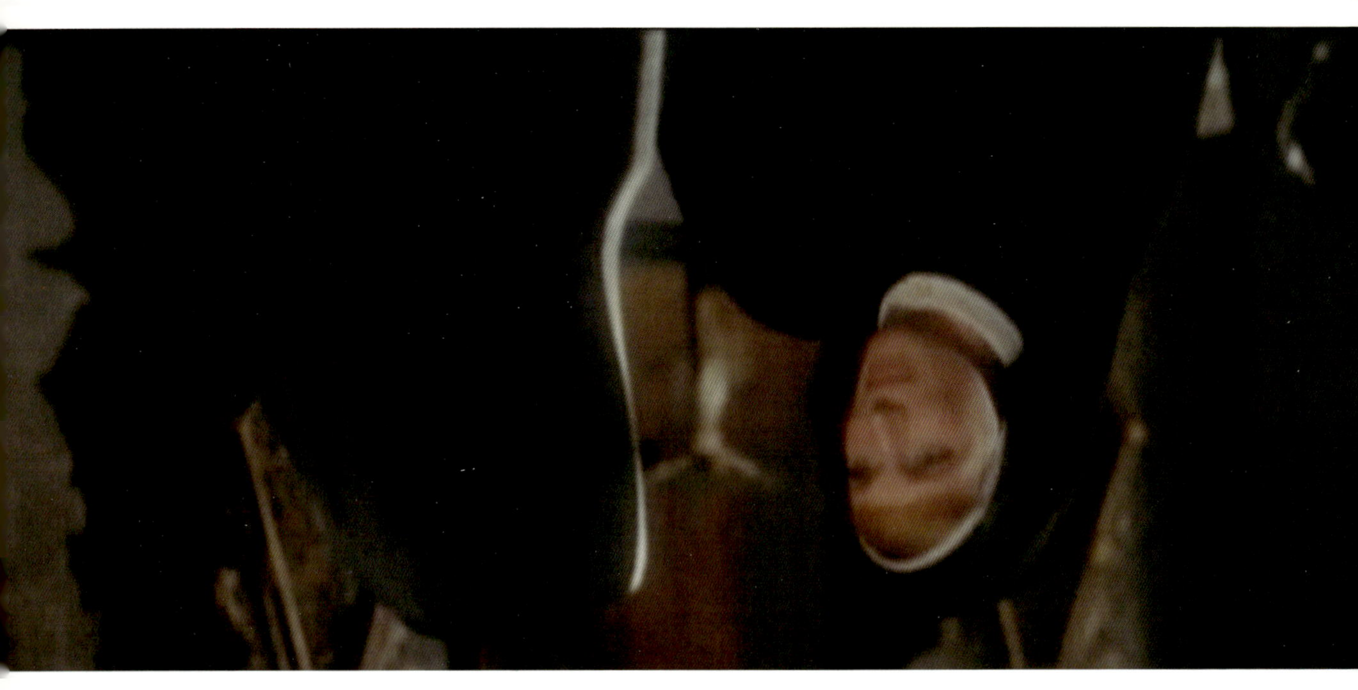

PAUL McCARTHY, *cisuM fo dnuoS ehT / The Sound of Music*, 2008 (still)

McCarthy's decision to literally overturn this uplifting narrative could be seen, in the first instance, as an attempt to plumb the cultural unconscious of a 1960s middlebrow generation. A symbolic prototype of familial unity, of wholesomeness, is subverted from within its own mechanical (filmic) matrix. This sets up parallels with Hiller's *An Entertainment.* Although Hiller's work ostensibly deals with the collective cultural imaginary of children over generations, as encoded in the popular imagery which they are submitted to, it took much of its immediate impetus from the anxieties felt by adults in relation to children at the turn of the 1990s. McCarthy arguably addresses this same generation of adults, along, of course, with their children (for whom *The Sound of Music* may already have the character of folklore).

Having said this, there was a very specific reason for McCarthy's decision to use this film for a work in 2001. The work was first shown in Austria in that year in response to the rise of Jörg Haider's Freedom Party, an extreme right-wing party with fascist sympathies which formed a coalition government in 2000 with Wolfgang Schüssel's People's Party, provoking massive opposition in Europe and elsewhere.[72] The latter half of the *The Sound of Music* centres on the escape of the von Trapp family from Austria as a result of their repudiation of Hilter's *Anschluss* and the entry of the Nazis into Austria. McCarthy's reversal of the film, at a time when fascist currents were again emerging in Austria, might be seen as ironically reversing the sentiments of the original plot. (Not surprisingly, the film has never been well-received in Austria, where it is seen as an American watering-down of Austrian culture, or in Germany, where its treatment of Nazism was considered problematic.)

But beyond this, *The Sound of Music* could be seen as a perfect vehicle for McCarthy, given his former preoccupations as an artist. He has already produced major video works, in collaboration with Mike Kelley, which subvert classic family/childhood tales (*Heidi* of 1991 and *Pinocchio Pipenose Householddilemma* of 1994). The repressed patriarch, Captain von Trapp, who dominates the middle section of the *The Sound of Music* (although in *cisuM fo dnuoS ehT* he is, of course, turned on his head) is the kind of figure who constantly emerges in McCarthy's art as an ogre or buffoon (as for instance in the *Grand Pop* performance of 1977). It is important also to realise that McCarthy has often been interested in his work in issues of formal and psychological disorientation vis-à-vis the spectator. British viewers of *cisuM fo dnuoS ehT* may well be reminded of Douglas Gordon's practice of slowing-down or reordering existing filmic structures (as in his *24 Hour Psycho* of 1993), but situations in which the spectator's visual or spatial expectations are reversed or dislocated have been longstanding features of McCarthy's work. Discussing several examples of installation, film and projection works by McCarthy from the 1970s to the present, which were shown in a recent major exhibition, Chrissie Iles talks of 'an almost ethical impulse' on McCarthy's part to 'question everything – to turn it upside down, see it from an opposite angle ... bring the viewer to a state of not knowing what is the "right" side up.'[73] This impulse is clearly apparent in *cisuM fo dnuoS ehT*. He savagely upends all of the famously reassuring and noble moments in the film; the singing of *My Favourite Things*, *Do-Re-Mi*, *Climb Every Mountain*, and so on. The film's protagonists hang like bats from the upper edge of the screen; the soundtrack, played backwards, is often deeply weird, like air being sucked through a tunnel. The effect, given all of the emotional baggage one brings to the film, is either hilarious, frustrating or highly disturbing.

Given the ideas that were presented at the beginning of this chapter, McCarthy's gesture might be seen as a perverse overlaying of an authorial sensibility onto a filmic text redolent of childhood innocence and family cohesion (in terms of what has been said about toys in recent art, this amounts to an overlaying of an adult's sensibility onto a child's). The argument of this exhibition is that it is this structural operation which characterises the late-twentieth century encounter between art and the things of childhood. This in turn reflects societal shifts whereby the child is increasingly conceptualised from a psychologistic viewpoint, such that the discourses of psychology or psychotherapy become integrated with, and inextricable from, the imagery of toys and play. With this in mind, I have attempted to trace a path from the essentially autobiographical works of Bourgeois and Chadwick, via the differently inflected forms of nostalgia in Gober and Koons, through to the direct incorporation of psychologistic modes in the work in Kelley, McCarthy and Hiller.

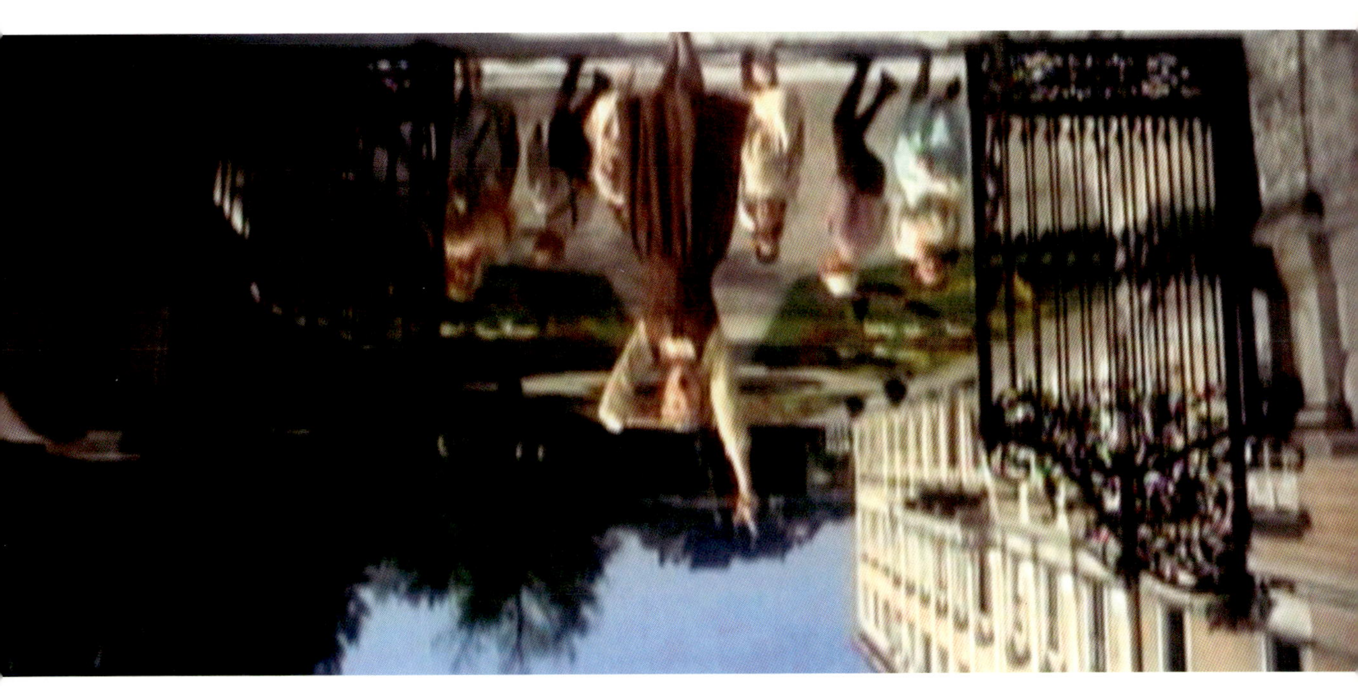

PAUL McCARTHY, *cisuM fo dnuoS ehT / The Sound of Music*, 2008 (still)

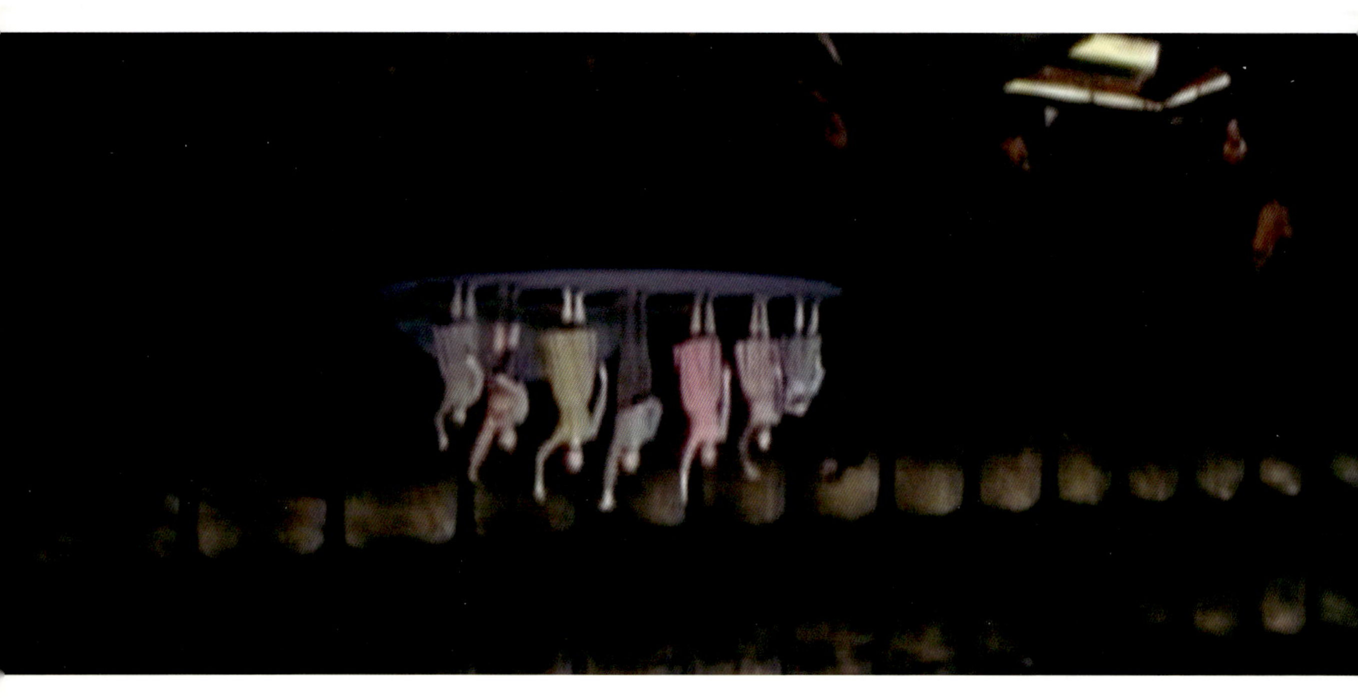

PAUL McCARTHY, *cisuM fo dnuoS ehT / The Sound of Music*, 2008 (still)

There are times, however, when it appears that the artist might be ironically adopting a regressive position; re-occupying, so to speak, the artist's child-self – as powerfully thematised in the works by Chadwick, Gober and Hiller. If 'Childish Things' has largely examined toy-like objects, it has done so with an eye to the way children's attitudes to toys, which can be bound up with dark and aggressive fantasies, are mimicked by artists. To return to my introductory remarks, the works in this show are 'toys for adults'. Perhaps more than anything McCarthy's aggressive iconoclasm in *cisuM fo dnuoS ehT* finally suggests a return to childish fantasies of omnipotence and destruction. Like an infant with its plaything, McCarthy probes the workings of the cultural artefact he has chosen. He takes us back to Baudelaire's brilliant description of the child at play: '(he) twists and turns his toy ... From time to time, he makes it re-start its mechanical motions, sometimes in the opposite direction. Its marvellous life comes to a stop. The child makes a supreme effort; at last he opens it up ... But *where is the soul*?'[74]

NOTES

62. Guy Brett, 'Susan Hiller's Shadowland', *Art In America*, April 1991, p. 142.
63. Susan Hiller in interview with Stuart Morgan, in *Susan Hiller*, Tate Publishing, London, 1996, p. 44.
64. Tony Sarg, 'Foreword', in John Payne Collier, *Punch and Judy: A Short History with the Original Dialogue*, Dover Publications, New York, 2006.
65. *Susan Hiller: Belshazzar's Feast*, Tate New Art / The Artist's View series, Tate Publishing, London, 1985, p. 13.
66. Hiller in interview with Stuart Morgan, op. cit., p. 45.
67. Ibid.
68. Susan Hiller as cited by Guy Brett in 'Susan Hiller's Shadowland', op. cit., p. 143.
69. 'Out of Bounds' in Lucy Lippard (ed.), *Susan Hiller* (exh. cat.), ICA, London, 1986, unpaginated.
70. Pauline Kael, *McCall's*, March, 1965.
71. Steven Askew, notes on 'The Sound of Music', *Metro*, date unknown.
72. See Federico Windhausen, 'Selected Shorts: 09.08.08' http://artforum.com/film/id=21069
73. Chrissie Iles, 'Preface' in *Paul McCarthy: Central Symmetrical Rotation Movement: Three Installations, Two Films* (exh. cat.), Whitney Museum of American Art, New York, 2008, p. 6.
74. Baudelaire, op. cit., see note 45.

LIST OF WORKS

LOUISE BOURGEOIS

pp. 18-19, 20
OEDIPUS, 2003
10 elements:
Fabric, stainless steel, wood, glass
177.8 x 182.8 x 91.4 cm

Courtesy Chaim & Read
and Hauser & Wirth

HELEN CHADWICK

pp. 26, 34
THE INCUBATOR, BIRTH
FROM *EGO GEOMETRIA SUM*, 1983
Photographic emulsion on plywood
15 x 27 x 45 cm

THE FONT, AGED 3 MONTHS
FROM *EGO GEOMETRIA SUM*, 1983
Photographic emulsion on plywood
23 x 50 x 50 cm

THE BOAT, AGED 3 YEARS
FROM *EGO GEOMETRIA SUM*, 1983
Photographic emulsion on plywood
24 x 38 x 91 cm

THE WIGWAM, AGED 5 YEARS
FROM *EGO GEOMETRIA SUM*, 1983
Photographic emulsion on plywood
89 x 79 x 79 cm

THE BED, AGED 6¾ YEARS,
FROM *EGO GEOMETRIA SUM*, 1983
Photographic emulsion on plywood
54 x 56 x 115 cm

Helen Chadwick Estate

pp. 28-29
THE JUGGLER'S TABLE
FROM *EGO GEOMETRIA SUM*, 1983
Tablecloth: black velvet; models:
photographic paper, card and glue
Tablecloth approx 120 cm diameter;
models (17 x 10 x 5.5 cm; 15 x 15 x 7 cm; 14 x 14 x 7 cm; 16 x 6.5 x 10.5 cm; 13.5 x 13.5 x 16 cm; 9 x 19 x 9 cm; 14.5 x 6.5 x 17.5 cm; 18 x 10 x 10 cm; 5.5 x 5.5 x 19.5 cm

Estate of Helen Chadwick
Henry Moore Institute /
Leeds Museums and Galleries

ROBERT GOBER

p. 40
PLAYPEN, 1986
Enamel paint on wood
66.5 x 99 x 99 cm

Daros Collection,
Switzerland

SUSAN HILLER

pp. 70–71, 73
AN ENTERTAINMENT, 1990
4 synchronized video programmes
25 min 59 secs

Tate: Purchased 1995

MIKE KELLEY

pp. 58
INNARDS, 1990
Blanket with stitched on toys
5 x 216 x 177 cm

Collection S.M.A.K.,
Stedelijk Museum voor Actuele
Kunst, Gent

JEFF KOONS

p. 44
WINTER BEARS, 1988
Polychromed wood
124.5 x 117 x 45 cm

Tate: Tate and National Galleries
of Scotland. Acquired jointly
through The d'Offay Donation with
assistance from the National Heritage
Memorial Fund and The Art Fund 2008

pp. 47, 95
BEAR AND POLICEMAN, 1988
Pigment on wood
215 x 110 x 83 cm

Kunstmuseum Wolfsburg

PAUL McCARTHY

p. 54
CHILDREN'S ANATOMICAL
EDUCATIONAL FIGURE, c. 1990
Fabric, wool; found object
172.7 x 129.5 x 116.8 cm

pp. 79, 80, 83, 84
CISUM FO DNUOS EHT /
THE SOUND OF MUSIC, 2008
Video
175 mins

Courtesy the artist
and Hauser & Wirth

BIBLIOGRAPHY

Agamben, Giorgio: *Stanzas: Word and Phantasm in Western Culture* trans. R. Martinez), University of Minnesota Press, Minneapolis, 1993

Agamben, Giorgio: *Infancy and History: On the Destruction of Experience* (1978) (trans. L. Heron), Verso, London and New York, 2007

Ariès, Philippe: *Centuries of Childhood* (1960) (trans. R. Baldrick), Peregrine Books, Harmondsworth, 1986

Barthes, Roland: *Mythologies* (1957) (trans. A. Lavers), Granada, London, 1981

Bätzner, Nike: *Faites vos jeux! Kunst und Spiel seit Dada:* (exh. cat.), Kunstmuseum Liechtenstein and Hatje Cantz, Ostfildern, 2005

Baudelaire, Charles: *The Painter of Modern Life and Other Essays* trans. J. Mayne), Da Capo Press, New York, 1964

Benjamin, Walter: *Walter Benjamin's Archive: Images, Texts and Signs* (eds U. Marx et al.), Verso, London and New York, 2007

Benjamin, Walter: *Selected Writings, Vol 2: 1927-1934*, (ed. M. W. Jennings, H. Eiland and G. Smith; trans. R. Livingstone et al.), Belknap Press, Cambridge, Massachusetts and London, 1999

Bernadac, Marie-Laure: *Louise Bourgeois*, Flammmarion, Paris, 2006

Bourgeois, Louise: *Destruction of the Father/Reconstruction of the Father: Writings and Interviews 1923-1997*, Violette Editions, London, 1998

Breton, André: *Surrealism and Painting* (trans. S. Watson Taylor), Icon Editions, New York, 1972

Brett, Guy (ed.): *Susan Hiller* (exh. cat.), Tate Publishing, London, 1996

Brown, Michèle: *The Little History of the Teddy Bear*, Sutton Publishing, Stroud, 2001

Brunner, Bernd: *Bears: A Brief History* (trans. L. Lantz), Yale University Press, New Haven and London, 2007

Caillois, Roger: *The Edge of Surrealism: A Roger Caillois Reader* (ed. C. Frank, trans. C. Frank and C. Naish), Duke University Press, Durham, 2003

Caillois, Roger: *Man, Play and Games* (1958) (trans. M. Barash), University of Illinois Press, Urbana and Chicago, 2001

Chadwick, Helen: *Enfleshings*, Secker and Warburg, London, 1989

Collier, John Payne: *Punch and Judy: A Short History with Original Dialogue*, Dover Publications, New York, 2006

Cross, Gary: *Kids' Stuff: Toys and the Changing World of American Childhood*, Harvard University Press, Cambridge, Massachusetts, 1997

Fass, Paula S. and Mason, Mary Ann (eds): *Childhood in America*, New York University Press, New York and London, 2000

Foster, Hal: *The Return of the Real: The Avant-Garde at the End of the Century*, The MIT Press, Cambridge, Massachusetts, 1996

Freud, Sigmund: *The Pelican Freud Library, vol. 14 (trans. A. Tyson)*, Penguin, Harmondsworth, 1985

Hiller, Susan: *The Provisional Texture of Reality: Selected Talks and Interviews 1977–2007* (ed. A. Kokoli), JRP Ringier, Zurich, 2008

Hopkins, David: *After Modern Art 1945–2000*, Oxford University Press, Oxford, 2000

Hopkins, David: *Dada's Boys: Identity and Play in Contemporary Art* (exh. cat.), The Fruitmarket Gallery, Edinburgh, 2006

Hopkins, David: *Dada's Boys: Masculinity After Duchamp*, Yale University Press, New Haven and London, 2007

Huizinga, Johan: *Homo Ludens*, Roy Publishers, Boston, 1950

Iles, Chrissie: *Paul McCarthy: Central Symmetrical Rotation Movement: Three Installations Two Films* (exh. cat.), Whitney Museum of American Art, New York, 2008

Kelley, Mike: *The Uncanny* (exh. cat.), Verlag der Buchhandlung Walther König, Cologne, 2004

Kellein, Thomas: *Mike Kelley* (exh. cat.), Kunsthalle Basel / Hatje Cantz, 1992

Lippard, Lucy (ed.): Susan Hiller (exh. cat.), Institute of Contemporary Art, London, 1986

Mavor, Carol *(ed.)*: *Reading Boyishly: Roland Barthes, J. M. Barrie, Jacques Henri Lartigue, Marcel Proust, and D. W. Winnicott*, Duke University Press, Durham, 2007

McCarthy, Paul: *Head Shop/Shop Head: Works 1966–2006* (exh. cat.), Stedl, Göttingen and Moderna Museet, Stockholm, 2006

Mitchell, Juliet (ed.): *The Selected Melanie Klein*, Peregrine Books, Harmondsworth, 1986

Morgan, Stuart and Morris, Frances: *Rites of Passage: Art for the End of the Century* (exh. cat.), Tate Publishing, London, 1995

Morris, Frances (ed.): *Louise Bourgeois* (exh. cat.), Tate Publishing, London, 2007

Morris, Frances: *Louise Bourgeois: Stitches in Time* (exh. cat.), August Projects, London and IMMA, Dublin, 2003

Robert Gober (exh. cat.), Museum Boijmans Van Beuningen, Rotterdam, 1990

Muthesius, Angelika (ed.): *Jeff Koons*, Taschen, Cologne, 1992

Nixon, Mignon: *Fantastic Reality: Louise Bourgeois and a Story of Modern Art*, The MIT Press, Cambridge, Massachusetts and London, 2005

Pilcher, Jane and Wagg, Stephen: *Thatcher's Children?: Politics, Childhood and Society in the 1980s and 1990s*, Falmer Press, London, 1996

Rugoff, Ralph et al.: *Paul McCarthy*, Phaidon Press, London, 1996

Sladen, Mark (ed.): *Helen Chadwick* (exh. cat.), Barbican Art Gallery, London and Hatje Cantz, Ostfildern, 2004

Stewart, Susan: *On Longing: Narratives of the Miniature, the Gigantic, the Souvenir, the Collection*, Duke University Press, Durham and London, 1993

Storr, Robert et al.: *Louise Bourgeois*, Phaidon Press, London, 2003

Sutton-Smith, Brian: *Toys as Culture*, Gardner Press, New York, 1986

Sutton-Smith, Brian: *The Ambiguity of Play*, Harvard University Press, Cambridge, Massachusetts, 1997

Varnedoe, Kirk and Gopnik, Adam: *High and Low: Modern Art and Popular Culture* (exh. cat.), The Museum of Modern Art, New York, 1990

Warner, Marina: *From the Beast to the Blonde: On Fairy Tales and their Tellers*, Chatto and Windus, London, 1994

Warner, Marina: *Only Make Believe: Ways of Playing* (exh. cat.), Compton Verney, 2004

Welchman, John C. et al.: *Mike Kelley*, Phaidon Press, London, 1999

Welchman, John C. : *Art After Appropriation: Essays on Art in the 1990s*, G+B Arts International, London, 2001

Welchman, John C. (ed.): *Mike Kelley: Minor Histories: Statements, Conversations, Proposals*, The MIT Press, Cambridge, Massachusetts and London, 2004

Winnicott, Donald W.: *Through Paediatrics to Psychoanalysis: Collected Papers* (1958), Karnac Books, London, 1984

Winnicott, Donald W.: *Playing and Reality* (1971), Pelican, Harmondswoth, 1988

ACKNOWLEDGEMENTS

DAVID HOPKINS THANKS

Aspects of the research for this publication have previously been presented on two occasions: at the Association of Art Historians Conference, University of Glasgow, April 2010, where I chaired a panel with Debbie Lewer titled 'Dada and Surrealism in Play', and at the 'Convulsive Nursery' conference at Manchester University in May 2010. I thank James Boaden for the invitation to speak on the latter occasion.

My special thanks go to Claire Sawyer, of the Henry Moore Institute in Leeds, who was extremely helpful in orientating me through the Helen Chadwick Archive and in making material available for publication. I am also grateful to Karin Seinsoth of Hauser and Wirth, Zürich, for facilitating my communication with Paul McCarthy, and to Susan Hiller for her comments on the project.

The staff of The Fruitmaket Gallery have been as friendly and imaginative as ever and I extend my warm thanks to them. I also thank Claudia Heide for her constant support, and my son, Ben, for sharing his toys with me.

PUBLICATION CREDITS

Authored by David Hopkins

Edited by Fiona Bradley
Designed and typeset
by Elizabeth McLean
Assisted by Samantha Woods

Printed by Stewarts of Edinburgh
Printed and bound in the UK

Distributed by Art Data
12 Bell Industrial Estate,
50 Cunnington Street
London, W4 5HB
Telephone +44 (0)20 8747 1061
www.artdata.co.uk

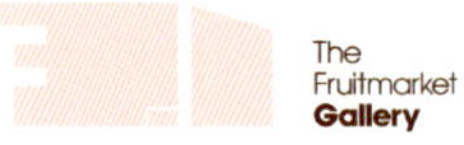

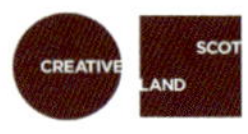

THE FRUITMARKET GALLERY

PICTURE CREDITS

cover, p.57: Courtesy the artist and Hauser & Wirth. p. 9, 47, 95 © Jeff Koons. pp. 18-19, 20 Courtesy Cheim & Read and Hauser & Wirth. Photo: Christopher Burke. p. 24 Photo © Edmund Engelman. pp. 26, 28-29, 30, 34, 35, 36 Leeds Museums & Galleries (Henry Moore Institute Archive). p. 33 © 2010. Digital image, The Museum of Modern Art, New York / Scala, Florence. p. 40 Daros Collection, Switzerland. Photo: Dominique Uldry, Berne. p. 43 Daros Collection, Switzerland. Photo: A. Burger, Zürich. p. 44 ARTIST ROOMS. Acquired jointly with the National Galleries of Scotland through The d'Offay Donation with assistance from the National Heritage Memorial Fund and The Art Fund 2008. p.54 Courtesy the artist and Hauser & Wirth. Photograph: Stefan Altenburger Photography Zürich. p.58 Collection S.M.A.K., Gent, Belgium. Photo: Dirk Pauwels. p. 61 Courtesy the artist and Metro Pictures. p.64 Courtesy Sonnabend Gallery. pp.70-71 Courtesy the artist and Matt's Gallery, London. p. 73 © Tate, London, 2010. p.74 © Victoria and Albert Museum, London. p. 77 Image courtesy Gimpel Fils. pp. 79, 80, 83, 84 Courtesy the artist and Hauser & Wirth

The Fruitmarket Gallery would like to thank all those who supplied photographs and have given permission to reproduce copyrighted material in this book. Every effort has been made to locate and credit copyright holders of the images reproduced in this book and the publisher welcomes communication from any copyright holder from whom permission was inadvertly not gained.

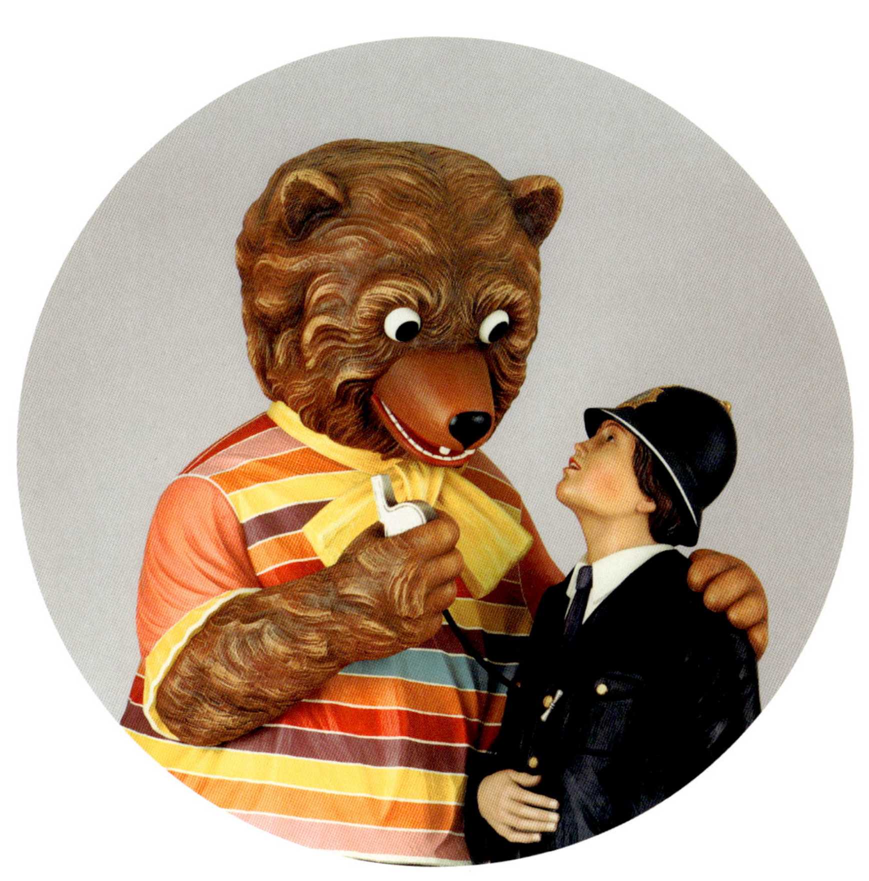